PRESENTATIONS

Business titles from Adams Media Corporation

ADAMS

PRESENTATIONS

Proven Techniques for Creating Presentations That Get Results

DARIA PRICE BOWMAN

Adams Media Corporation
Holbrook, Massachusetts

This is a *CWL Publishing Enterprises Book*, developed by John A. Woods
for Adams Media Corporation. For more information, contact CWL Publishing
Enterprises at 3010 Irvington Way, Madison, WI 53713-3414, (608) 273-3710.

Published by
Adams Media Corporation
260 Center Street, Holbrook, MA 02343

ISBN: 1-55850-798-1

Printed in the United States of America.

J I H G F E

Bowman, Daria Price.
    The presentation handbook : how to prepare and make winning
presentations / Daria Price Bowman.
        p.   cm.
    Includes index.
    ISBN 1-55850-798-1
    1. Business presentations. 2. Business presentations—Audio-visual aids.
3. Public speaking. I. Title.
    HF5718.22.B69   1998
    658.4'5—dc21   97-30456
                                                                            CIP

This publication is designed to provide accurate and authoritative information
with regard to the subject matter covered. It is sold with the understanding that
the publisher is not engaged in rendering legal, accounting, or other professional
advice. If legal advice or other expert assistance is required, the services of a
competent professional person should be sought.
    — From a *Declaration of Principles* jointly adopted by a Committee of the
American Bar Association and a Committee of Publishers and Associations

This book is available at quantity discounts for bulk purchases.
For information, call 1-800-872-5627 (in Massachusetts, 781-767-8100).

Visit our home page: www.adamsmedia.com
Visit our exciting small business website: www.businesstown.com

To my family for believing in me

Contents

Preface

When I was asked to write a book about giving presentations, I thought, "This is great. It'll be cake. After all, I've been making presentations for twenty years. I know all about presentations." After just a few days at the computer, I saw it wasn't cake at all. In fact, I realized that without doing tons of research, I was toast. My presentation expertise was based mostly on seat-of-the-pants experience. With the exception of a day of media instruction, I made all those presentations with no other specific training and, truth be known, not a great deal of planning.

In hindsight, I now know that my success in giving presentations was based on an intimate and complete understanding of my subject matter. I had been presenting *my* programs, *my* ideas, *my* house museum (well, it was in my care anyway!), and *my* garden experiences. I was also able to succeed because of a combination of my enthusiasm for the subject matter, a knack for sales, an enjoyment for being "on stage," and more than just a little dumb luck.

I hope this book will help those who are smart enough to approach giving a presentation rationally and intelligently— rather than by the seat of their pants—by drawing on the expertise of successful professionals who know why some things work and others don't. I am grateful for all the research and experience of those professionals who are quoted in the following pages.

And I owe a debt of gratitude to a number of people who helped me:

First I want to thank John Woods for trusting me with the job of writing this book. Heartfelt thanks go to my friend, neighbor, and reader Kay Holmes; to my e-mail experts Art Steinmark and Micky Melchiondo; to Beth Kauffman, who planned my media training, and Holly Severino, who helped me hone those skills; to my friends who shared their presentation experiences and expertise, including Eric Sauter, Maureen Shortt, Gena Ciccone, Pat Ciccone, Tom McKearn, Robert Grumet, Dave Roberts, Joe Luccaro, David Anderson, Matt Mason, Tia Faroud, Tim Conniff, and David Fredrickson; and to my father, Carl Price, for his language lore.

And I offer special and fond thank-yous to my husband Ernie and daughters Sam and Cassie, who lived with the piles of books and reprints, the hasty dinners, and my more-or-less emotional absence while I struggled with the research and writing.

Introduction

Some people are actually more afraid of public speaking than they are of dying. In fact, according to *The Book of Lists* by David Wallenchinsky, Irving Wallace, and Ann Wallace, the fear of public speaking is the most common fear, surpassing the fear of flying, snakes, spiders, heights, and even death.

There are those for whom just the thought of standing up in front of a group will make their palms sweat, their hair curl, their stomach churn and their heart lurch. If you are one of those people, the following pages will help you identify the cause of that fear, break it down into manageable pieces, and conquer it. This book will also show you how to use the right ingredients to plan and execute a successful presentation.

If you are only mildly uncomfortable with the idea of making a presentation, but haven't a clue about where to start in the process, this book is also for you. It will show you how to define your audience and the strategies needed to reach them; to organize your material in a cohesive, sensible, and powerful format; to make logistical decisions and arrangements; to build rapport, use humor and drama, and involve your audience; to develop and use audio and visual aids; to improve the quality of your voice and make a good physical impression; to deal with distractions; to make presentations in special situations such as television interviews; to make in-house video presentations; and to make presentations to the elderly or to children.

Please don't feel confined to reading this book chapter by chapter. You may already know all about different presentation formats but be clueless when it comes to visuals. If that's your situation, skip Chapter 2 and turn immediately to Chapter 6, where you'll learn about charts, overheads, slides, videos, computer generated graphics, and the value of props and tangible objects in making a point.

If you're an expert at putting together computer-generated slides, but don't know the first thing about setting up a meeting room, go directly to Chapter 4, where you'll learn whether you should use a classroom or a U-shaped setup for your presentation.

While you are reading, it may help to keep in mind that presentations are as old as history. You are not the first person losing sleep over next week's presentation. And you're far from the only person who has ever had to worry about a less-than-perfect voice.

One of the earliest recorded presentations may very well have been when Moses presented the Ten Commandments to his people. This was apparently not an easy thing for Moses to do: "Moses said unto the Lord, 'O my Lord, I am not eloquent, neither heretofore, nor since thou has spoken unto thy servant: but I am slow of speech, and of a slow tongue'" (Exodus 2). It seems that Moses may have had a biblical case of stage fright.

Some presentations are more memorable than others. Houston Peterson, a chronicler of historic speeches, wrote in *A Treasury of the World's Greatest Speeches*: "If one were forced to put the history of public address into a preposterous nutshell, one might say that it began with some kind of leader charming, calming or exciting a responsive audience with spontaneous verbal magic." You might not be a spontaneous verbal magician, but with good preparation, you can still effectively inform, if not charm, your audience. Helping you do that is what this book is about.

One

Types of Presentations

Presentations come in nearly as many forms as there are life situations. In the business world, there are sales presentations, informational and motivational presentations, first encounters, interviews, briefings, status reports, image-building "dog and pony shows," and, of course, the inevitable training sessions.

Although we most often think of presentations in a business meeting context, there are countless occasions when that is not the case. For example, a church vestry presents the need for a capital fund-raising campaign to the congregation; a school district superintendent presents a program to parents about the introduction of foreign-language instruction in the elementary schools; an artist demonstrates decorative painting techniques to a group of interior designers; a horticulturist shows garden club members or homeowners how they might use native plants in the suburban landscape; a police officer addresses a neighborhood association about initiating a safety program; a homeowner presents a proposal for an addition to his home requiring a variance to the municipal zoning board; and a self-help expert presents a video (for $49.99 plus shipping and handling) about how "you too can become a millionaire."

Presentations can also be categorized as vocational and avocational. In addition, they are expository or persuasive. And they can be impromptu, extemporaneous, written, or memorized.

But when looking at presentations in the broadest terms, perhaps it's more important to focus on their purpose. Kitty O. Locker, of Ohio State University, points out in *Business and Administrative Communication* that there are three basic purposes for giving oral presentations:

- To inform
- To persuade
- To build goodwill

INFORMATIVE PRESENTATIONS

Scott Ober, of Ball State University, the author of *Contemporary Business Communications*, divides informative presentations into two distinct categories—reporting and explaining. He says that the reporting presentation brings the audience up to date on projects or events, telling how things are going. These situations might include shareholders' meetings, executive briefings, or oral sales reports. The explanatory presentation provides information about products and procedures, rules and regulations, operations, and other nitty-gritty data.

Informational presentations include talks, seminars, proposals, workshops, conferences, and meetings where the presenter or presenters share their expertise, and information is exchanged. In a business format, it might be a supervisor explaining new forms, products, regulations, or filing procedures to employees. During the sales process, the salesperson may provide information on the product or service to a prospective customer. In a retail situation, newly hired sales clerks may attend a presentation on selling techniques or loss prevention. And in an educational setting, an informative presentation may report on changes in the reading curriculum.

PERSUASIVE PRESENTATIONS

These are the presentations in which you attempt to convince the audience to buy your product or service, to support your goals or concepts, or to change their minds or attitudes. Persuasive presentations, which are sometimes called transactional, are often motivational. For example, during a sermon a priest might attempt to persuade the congregation to accept the teachings of the church in order to reduce racial tensions. Or a college dorm proctor, during a presentation to new freshmen, may try to motivate the students in her care to avoid drugs, alcohol, and unprotected sex.

In a business context, a supervisor may make a presentation on teamwork in order to motivate employees to support new cooperative efforts within the company structure. It may be a situation in which the board is asking the shareholders to support changes in the way dividends are distributed. It could be that the distribution arm of an organization is making suggestions about packaging changes that would reduce shipping costs. Or perhaps the marketing department is trying to sell top management on a new promotional campaign.

GOODWILL PRESENTATIONS

We've all seen this kind of presentation. Every year, the fire company in my little town has an awards night at which key members are honored for their service. And the library has an annual community service recognition dinner at which local leaders are praised. Schools, soccer teams, and country clubs have awards banquets to recognize the top competitors. Companies honor retirees with a dinner. At special ceremonies, outgoing presidents of civic and charitable organizations are given plaques for their years of service. Departments, units, or teams within a business organization are often rewarded for their success at meetings at which their work is showcased. Each of these events usually includes some kind of presentation, most often in the form of a speech and sometimes with a slide show, video, or multimedia event.

Goodwill presentations, which often take the form of after-dinner speeches, are often designed to be entertaining—for example, by sharing video highlights of the football or tennis season or anecdotes from the president's ten years at the helm, by recounting the town's recreational program from its early years to the present, or by "roasting" the top salesperson. Sometimes they are ceremonial—for example, when inducting a new officer, dedicating a memorial plaque, presenting an award, or delivering a eulogy.

The purpose of goodwill presentations is pretty obvious. That purpose is to build goodwill, to make people feel good about themselves, and to build respect for the organization and/or the product, as well as for peers, colleagues, and superiors.

MULTIPURPOSE PRESENTATIONS

Presentations, however, usually have more than one purpose. A presentation to employees may be announced as an informative session on new regulations, but in fact may also be an all-out effort to persuade workers to buy into the new rules.

An introductory presentation about new software programs may be a not-so-subtle nudge to employees who have been slow to become computer literate. The fire department's awards banquet may indeed recognize the hard work of its members, but it may also represent an attempt to raise funds and recruit new volunteers. The library's gala community recognition night may coincide with its annual fund-raising campaign. And the informative presentation that reports the status of a sports sponsorship public relations program may be an attempt to persuade the powers that be to increase the funding for the project.

Now that we understand what presentations are in their broadest terms, let's look at specific presentation situations.

SALES

Probably the single largest category of presentations is the sales scenario. Though throughout life we are "selling" ourselves to teachers, prospective mates, neighbors, or colleagues, in the business world, we are most often selling our products, services, or ideas.

Sales presentations can start out simply as *first encounters*—those one-on-one get-to-know-each-other meetings over lunch or a no-frills quickie meeting in a prospective client's office. If things go according to plan, your first encounter might progress to a full-blown sales presentation with the top brass, the entire sales team, and a multimedia show. But chances are, you'll just schedule a follow-up meeting at which you will present your proposal and position yourself to close the deal.

Though sales techniques are complex (and a subject for another book), two essentials for success in a sales presentation are knowing and understanding your audience, and building rapport. These areas are addressed in Chapter 2.

TRAINING

In training sessions, presenters teach participants a variety of skills. Topics might include:

- Sales techniques
- How to deal with diversity in the workplace
- Time management and stress reduction
- Team building
- Negotiation or leadership
- Meetings management
- How to give presentations

And that's only the beginning. Some companies have entire divisions devoted to training, with course catalogs as thick as the Sunday *New York Times*.

Outside the realm of the business world, the choices are even broader. One might attend training sessions on subjects ranging from yoga to gardening to French conversation to wallpaper hanging to MS-DOS to Bible study. In and out of the business world, people are more and more looking for ways to balance their lives, and they find that attending various training sessions is one of the routes they can travel to reach their personal goals.

In many business situations, training is a captive situation (see Chapter 2 about types of audiences) in which the audience has no choice but to participate. In order to reach the audience, the presenter must make a connection and build rapport, just as in a sales situation.

In the realm of self-improvement and creative or fun training sessions, participants are often the self-actualized types who are looking for fulfillment and entertainment. These folks, as you will learn in Chapter 2, are a pleasure to present to.

ENTERTAINMENT

This type of presentation is often designed to serve more than one purpose. It may be planned to inform, build a positive image, and create goodwill. For example, an after-dinner talk at a museum's fund-raising event may focus on recent acquisitions, but may also be designed to thank current donors and to place the museum in a positive light in the minds of prospective donors.

Entertaining presentations are often scheduled by clubs, service organizations, adult education programs, and social organizations as part of their weekly or monthly meetings. They are also frequently included in the activities schedules for retirement communities.

POLITICAL ARENA

Presentations in the political arena are primarily grouped in the persuasive category. But to be effective, they must include lots of information and also build goodwill.

Who can forget the sight of Ross Perot making his balanced budget presentations, complete with easel-mounted bar graphs and pie charts? He offered more information than most of us could absorb, and some people found him entertaining. But was he persuasive? Not very!

Bill Clinton is famous for his comfy, personalized presentations featuring real people with real-life stories to tell. He generates lots of goodwill, is very persuasive, but is not always informative.

Jesse Jackson makes memorable presentations that include no props or fancy staging, but are built simply on an oratory style lifted right from the pulpit. Persuasive? Informative? Goodwill generators? You decide.

In our media-crazed society where every move is televised for all the world to see, political presentations take on gigantic proportions. Most politicians running in major market races call on professional political consultants to manage their public (and private, in many cases) appearances so that they present the right image for each audience, deliver the right message in the right context and format, and develop the right rapport with each audience segment.

Because the electorate is complex and heterogeneous, a politician working at the city, state, or national level will most likely need to have several presentation styles and messages in his bag of tricks in order to win over the diverse audiences. At the small-town municipal or county level, politics are no less complicated but don't tend to include the same type of political consultant assistance. A candidate should have a pretty good idea of who his or her audience is and should tailor the presentation to the "What's in it for me?" factor, as described in Chapter 2.

IMAGE BUILDING

Image building is a something of a catchall category because it covers so much ground. These presentations can be, at once, informative, entertaining, certainly goodwill-oriented, and, of course, persuasive.

Often in the realm of public relations and marketing professionals, an image-building presentation represents an effort to position a company, an organization, or an individual as a leader in an industry or field, as an expert on a certain subject, as a good-guy, or as a good neighbor. In the end, however, most image-building work is tied to some kind of sales effort—whether it's selling a product, a service, a person, or a concept. And image-building presentations will frequently be used as launching pads for extensive public relations publicity efforts.

A chemical company may ask one of its scientists to make a presentation to a high school chemistry class on the positive role chemicals play in our daily lives. This makes the chemical company look like a good neighbor and works toward alleviating negative impressions that could affect sales. Such a visit is almost always accompanied by an extensive public relations effort to generate publicity.

A doll manufacturer may address a national parenting organization on the issue of positive role models for girls in order to build the image of caring and responsibility. Here again the PR folks will be busy sending out press releases and trying to set up interview opportunities linked to the presentation.

Or a wanna-be political type may be found presenting his ideas on Medicare to a group of retirees, to position himself as a friend of senior citizens. His press secretary will have notified the media well in advance.

One of the clients I served when I worked in the public relations department of a large advertising agency was a trade association representative for the diaper service industry. Her job was to make image-building presentations around the country, positioning cloth diapers as a superior substitute for the disposable type. Whenever and wherever she spoke, my job was to schedule television and radio appearances and newspaper interviews in that market.

And another client, the 7-Eleven Corporation, held regional meetings at which elaborately staged multimedia presentations were given for the benefit of franchisees and their employees. The purpose was to maintain the company's positive image and to inspire franchisee loyalty. In this case the audience was limited to franchisees, not to the general public, so there was no need to alert the media.

Image-building presentations take many forms, running the gamut from simple, sincere speeches in a classroom to sound-and-light multimedia shows in giant auditoriums.

MOTIVATIONAL PRESENTATIONS

Here's another far-reaching category. Political candidates may give motivational presentations to their volunteer staffers to keep their level of commitment high. Spiritual leaders, of course, give motivational talks or sermons. A superintendent of schools may make a presentation to the district's teachers in order to motivate them to think of themselves as teachers first, union members second. A real-estate broker may bring in a motivational expert to help his staff get out of a sales slump. And then there are the self-help types, like those whose videos fill TV airtime on Saturday mornings with get-rich-quick schemes.

Motivation is another form of persuasion, but one that somehow takes on a more fervent, highly charged tone. Motivational presenters must know what makes the audience tick and zero in on their hot buttons. They also must use high-energy presenting tactics in order to capture the audience's attention for the entire message.

INTERVIEWS

When a company spokesperson, political candidate, writer, artist, inventor, or other expert appears on a radio or television talk show or is interviewed for a magazine or newspaper article, that person is making a presentation. This special aspect of presentations is covered in Chapter 10.

A job interview is yet another presentation form, one where the presenter should make an effort to identify her immediate audience (the interviewer), but also take great pains to know as much as possible about the larger audience (the company). Strategies for understanding the audience are discussed in Chapter 2.

AN ACADEMIC APPROACH

As part of their English curriculum, Matt Mason and his prep-school classmates were taught how to make a speech. Their text-book was a slim volume, published in 1950, entitled *The Speaker's Abstract: A Guide for Public Speaking* by Wilbur S. Howell of Princeton University.

Undoubtedly not the students' favorite subject, the public-speaking study covered some pretty dry ground. The preface of the text includes these pithy phrases:

> *Most of the time which a student has available for his training in speech-making should be spent in prepar-ing and delivering speeches of his own. Not only does he find this the most interesting part of his training; he finds also that, in the long run it is most valuable to him. His own experience before audiences, and the criticisms he receives on his speeches from his teach-ers and listeners, build up in his mind a system of experimental rhetorical principles, and these are all the better because they relate to the facts of speaking as he himself has observed them.*
>
> *This Abstract is designed to enable the student to learn some of the basic concepts that relate to the practice of speech-making, without making those con-cepts so detailed that they become a substantial com-petitor for the time he would otherwise be likely to spend upon the preparation and rehearsal of his speeches.*

Despite the fact that these words were written in unabashedly sexist language (after all, why, in 1950 when this was written, would females need to learn how to give a speech?) and that the tone is a bit pedagogical, the boys who took this course were better prepared than most to meet the challenges facing them in adulthood.

Though Wilbur S. Howell's little book hasn't been in print for decades, it offers valuable information and advice for anyone preparing a formal speech. He says, "A speech is an instrument which the speaker uses to get certain things done. He can't build a bridge with a speech. But by a speech he can enlist the support and cooperation that will enable him to get the bridge built. Support, consent, cooperation, willingness, consensus, agreement, acceptance, understanding—these terms indicate real things that can be said to be true of groups after speeches have been made to them."

Chances are that after writing and rewriting speeches, and then delivering them to their classmates and teachers, Matt Mason and his classmates were less likely to suffer from debilitating stage fright. How lucky they were to take that course!

Two

Know Your Audience

There are apathetic, sleeping audiences that must be awakened; there are hostile audiences that must be defied and conquered; there are alienated or sullen audiences that must be won back; there are frightened audiences that must be calmed. There are loyal, affectionate audiences that must be further inspired. There are cool, skeptical audiences that must be coolly convinced. There are heterogeneous audiences that must be moulded into some kind of unity.

—HOUSTON PETERSON

There are far more types of audiences than there are types of presentations because audiences are made up of people and people come in innumerable flavors. Suppose you are a scientist studying global warming, and you've become a recognized authority on the subject. You could be invited to speak to groups all across the country. What you say and how you say it depends on the makeup of those groups. You might be asked to address a roomful of factory operations managers who have no choice but to attend your talk, or you may go before a congressional committee looking into various environmental issues. An environmental group made up of people who are devoted to slowing the decline of the ozone layer might include your presentation on global warming at its annual convention. An international affairs group—in which the audience could be far more heterogeneous than many other groups—might ask you to speak at one of their meetings. And it's possible that Ted Koppel will interview you on *Nightline* one night and Katie Couric will schedule you for the next morning on the *Today* show.

You, the global warming expert, are likely to have several potential audiences—students, teachers, and fellow scientists come quickly to mind. And for each one of these types of audiences you will have to package your presentation differently. Of course, in any group, even those that appear to be homogeneous, there is likely to be some diversity in education, socioeconomic rank, age, political inclination, emotional state, or intellectual level, among other variables.

In the next few pages are profiles of types of audiences, strategies for identifying them, and tactics for reaching them effectively.

AUDIENCES

When you stand up to deliver a presentation before an audience, it's essential that you know who they are, why they are there, what specifically they expect to get from your presentation, and how they will react to your message. You won't always be able to determine all these factors, but you should try to gather as much background information as possible before your presentation. There will be times, especially with presentations that are open to the public, when you will only be able to guess.

Audiences can be classified into four basic categories:

- Captives
- Pragmatists
- Socially motivated
- Committed

Captives

People in a captive audience have no choice—they have to attend your presentation. It may be a required training session for managers addressing the issue of diversity, or a group of dentists picking up their continuing education credits, or a program on sexual harassment mitigation for military personnel. Teachers participating in an in-service day, students attending a mandatory assembly, factory workers learning about a new assembly process, or senior citizens participating in a retirement community orientation meeting might all fall under the category of captives.

Members of a captive audience are often called prisoners, especially in the lexicon of corporate trainers. Prisoners may or may not want to attend your presentation. Some participants will be happy just to be away from their desks for an hour or two. They may not be very motivated to receive your message, but they aren't likely to be hostile or negative.

Other captives may resent the intrusion your presentation makes on their already overloaded day. Or they may be angry over the fact that they don't have the power to not attend. As the presenter, you need to know what kind of pressure to be in your audience was put on attendees. Captives can be one of the most difficult types of audiences to address. Your presentation to a captive audience will require extra attention to delivery strategies, more energy, and perhaps an extra dose of humor, along with an unimpeachable command of your subject matter.

Pragmatists

A pragmatic audience has a different point of view. These are people who may have some say in whether they will attend your presentation. Perhaps your presentation is part of a two-session professional meeting with a choice of two or three talks per session. So the audience can pick one talk from column A and one from column B.

The people who select your presentation may be required to be at the meeting but have some leeway in how they spend their time there. This audience, though captive, is less likely to feel hostile and negative about you and your subject because, after all, they chose your talk on time management over someone else's presentation on stress reduction.

Pragmatic audiences aren't necessarily captives, however. Their motivation for attending your presentation may come from the desire or necessity to learn about your topic for their sales efforts, advancement, certification or recertification, continuing education, or just the need to keep current in their field or yours.

Pragmatists make excellent audiences for presentations that report, explain, and inform. Tell them what they need to know, and they'll be happy. Do it in a way that also entertains, and they'll be that much more receptive to your message.

Socially Motivated Audiences

Socially motivated audiences can be divided into two subgroups—those who are motivated to support a cause and those who are motivated by belonging to a group.

The cause-supporters will attend your presentation on the working conditions of migrant crop pickers because they advocate reforms in labor laws or because they support tighter immigrant worker regulations. Individuals in the audience who are sitting side by side can be for you or agin' you. This is a tough situation, and you should be prepared in advance with strategies for hostile questions, disruptive behaviors, or even heckling. This situation is discussed in some detail in the section entitled "Difficult Audiences."

Those who support your cause make up the dream audience. They will hang on your every word, will clap loudly and enthusiastically at your key points, and will ask questions that reinforce your message. Presenting to these folks will be a pleasure.

If, however, you expect a large number of hostile people in your audience, it may be a good idea to follow an old theatrical custom—paper the house. That means you fill as many seats as you can with your supporters so you won't be faced with an entirely negative audience. Politicians do this all the time, and it can be very effective, though it takes skillful orchestration.

Socially motivated audiences who attend a presentation because they are part of a group are open to all kinds of messages. Examples include senior citizen groups or area women's club members who will attend a presentation on historic preservation legislation one month and a travelogue on Kenya the next; or the local Rotary that will invite the community college president to speak about displaced worker retraining at the September meeting, followed in October by the head of the community arts association whose presentation looks at theater programs for children and youth.

For socially motivated participants, the message is not as crucial as the act of being in the audience among friends, acquaintances, colleagues, and peers. This audience is almost always easy to work with because their expectations are reasonable—they would like a little information presented in an entertaining and congenial manner.

Committed Audiences

Audience members who fall under the category of committed will attend your presentation because they really want to be there and hear what you have to say. Like the pragmatists, these are people searching for information that will help them increase sales, improve productivity, expand their client base, or raise their standard of living. They differ from pragmatists in that they have a higher level of enthusiasm for the topic.

A talk on pension planning, for example, will provide valuable information to those who need to achieve a certain level of security or comfort. A presentation on techniques for organizing a home office is like an answered prayer to an overwhelmed sole proprietor. And a talk on closing the deal may be exactly what an inexperienced salesperson is looking for.

Other committed audiences function at an even higher level of need—they may be hoping to attain competence or success through your presentation. Or they may be in the highly motivated and self-actualized population interested in doing things for the challenge or for the intellectual stimulation. These people are more likely to be the high achievers—at least in some parts of their lives.

Higher level committed types may seek out speakers and presentations on subjects that greatly interest them. They may, for example, attend all-day workshops on garden design because gardening is what they enjoy doing most. They may travel to hear an expert speak on innovations in yacht design. Or they may seek out a speaker who really understands the nuances of the situation in Albania. These people want to know everything there is to know about the subject, and they are a joy for the prepared presenter.

STRATEGIES FOR DEFINING YOUR AUDIENCE

Before you plan your presentation, you have to define your audience. The following checklist will help you do this:

- *What is the size of the group?*
  The number of people in your audience will affect your delivery style, the way you present visuals, the number and type of handouts, and the level of audience interaction.
- *What is the age distribution of the audience?*
  This is especially important if the audience is primarily made up of the very young or the very old. And age can make a difference in terms of reference points. For example, baby boomers will identify with references to the Vietnam War or Woodstock, whereas their parents will relate to references to the Korean War or Frank Sinatra.

- *Is the audience mostly men, mostly women, or mixed?*
  Though, in many cases, your content and delivery would be the same with either sex, there may be nuances that are more suitable for one group or the other. And you may have to work especially hard on your delivery style and your choice of words if your audience is made up entirely of the opposite sex. (Refer to the section on bias-free language in Chapter 7 for more information on this subject.)

- *How do audience members rank within their organization? And in relation to your position?*
  This is an especially important question when addressing members of a hierarchical organization such as a corporation, university, board of directors, or committee. If you are addressing a group of your superiors, you may need to work on building your confidence. But if you are speaking to people in lower ranks, you may have to guard against sounding condescending or arrogant.

- *Why are people attending your presentation?*
  Are they captives, socially or financially motivated, committed, or pragmatists?

- *How familiar are audience members with your topic?*
  If your subject is computer applications for the garden center and nursery trades, for example, it would be helpful to know what percentage of your audience uses computers already and at what level of sophistication. You would start from a different point of view for a group of novices from the point you would use for a group in which 90 percent of the nursery managers used computers for inventory and irrigation control, pesticide applications, and invoicing.

- *What is the level of education of audience members?*
  Your delivery will be markedly different for an audience made up of MBAs or PhDs from delivery for an audience made up of artists, engineers, or people who have only completed high school.

- *What kind of reaction to your message can you expect?*
  On hearing your announcement of downsizing plans, an audience whose jobs are secure will have a reaction dramatically different from one whose jobs are at risk. Residents at a town meeting are likely to react more enthusiastically to a presentation on plans to build a recreation center for their children than they are to one on plans to build a quarry.

The more you know about your audience's value systems, beliefs, experiences, and needs, along with demographic factors such as age, economic status, education, and age, the better able you will be to construct a successful presentation.

WHAT'S IN IT FOR ME?

It's a basic fact that audiences want and expect presenters to succeed, unless you are an ogre and they know it. Along with their expectation of your success lies another basic fact. It doesn't matter how generous, caring, giving, altruistic, or even saintly your audience members may be, chances are the question on their minds as they walk into your presentation is "What's in it for me?" It's human nature.

The "What's in it for me?" factor is so pronounced and widespread, it has its own acronym: WIIFM. By keeping in mind your audience's WIIFM needs, especially as you answer the questions in the "define your audience" checklist, you improve your chances of making a winning presentation.

Much has been written about the psychological makeup of motivated individuals and categorizing them according to Maslow's hierarchy of needs, a complicated and highly academic description of levels of needs (described as basic, safety, belonging, ego-status, and self-

---

actualization) on which a presenter might define the audience. The belief is that people must satisfy one level of need before going on to the next one.

There are drawbacks to using Maslow's descriptions, however. Because individuals are so complex, it's nearly impossible to categorize an entire audience based on rank or level of achievement, short of a personal interview for each member. And in this age of restructuring and automation, those considered to have achieved the ego-status or self-actualization levels may be striving once again to meet their safety needs. So, rather than getting bogged down in trying to determine where to categorize your audience according to Maslow, it might be better to ask some basic questions, gather as much information as you can, and then go with your instincts.

WHO'S IN CHARGE?

> *Even a nod from a person who is esteemed is of more force than a thousand arguments or studied sentences from others.*
>
> PLUTARCH

Scott Ober, the author of *Contemporary Business Communication*, stresses the importance of identifying the key decision maker in the audience. This person (and sometimes there is more than one) is often the highest ranking member of the audience. But sometimes the opinion leaders of a group aren't obvious at first.

For example, a board of directors may be led in theory by its chairman or president, but the person who really pulls the strings may be a former board president who now is simply a board member. In another arena, corporate officers may defer all decisions to the company attorneys. And in other organizations, the person who actually calls the shots may remain behind the scenes, relying on front line sources for vital information.

In one not-for-profit organization I know of, the director, staff, and trustees can't seem to make a move without the approval of a *former* board member who still calls the shots, though she's in her eighties and not very up to date in some of her thinking. If you can't convince her, you'll get nowhere with the rest of the members. On the other hand, if she likes what you have to say, you've got it made.

If your presentation is to people within your own organization, you should already know who makes decisions and directs opinions. If you don't, make it a priority to find out. If you are an outsider, you'll need to do a little digging to identify the key decision maker. Then, by understanding the expectations and needs of that person and addressing them in your presentation, you improve your chances for a positive reception to your message.

The best way of finding out who the opinion leaders and decision makers are in a company is to ask the person who has asked you to speak. Try to get as much detail as possible. Secretaries and administrative or executive assistants are often very astute in understanding how the hierarchy works at their firms, and can be valuable sources of information, too.

If you will be speaking to a well-known or publicly traded company, do a little research on the Internet, in back issues of the *Wall Street Journal*, and in other business publications. There are likely to be certain names that keep popping up that will give you some clues. Finally, use your networking skills to pinpoint where decisions are made within the firm. The extra effort will probably be worth the time.

When my partner and I developed a presentation for a promotional campaign for a bank, we were under the impression that the branch manager could give us the go-ahead to implement the plan. After weeks of stalling, she finally told us her boss had nixed our proposal. Eventually we discovered she never had the authority to develop the campaign and was simply hoping she could talk him into the plan. Rather than admit her predicament (because she was embarrassed for asking us to create the plan in the first place), she avoided us.

Straightaway, we should have asked the branch manager for the name of the person responsible for approving the plan. Thus, we would have understood the situation and, in all likelihood, would have turned the project down, saving us considerable time and a lot of irritation.

DIFFICULT AUDIENCES

Chances are you won't have the misfortune of confronting a hostile audience, but there may be a time when you will come up against a difficult situation. This is more apt to happen during a question-and-answer period than during the talk itself.

Sometimes the difficulty can take the form of a negative question from someone who disagrees with you. Or a person with a strong bias may ask a question that is really more a statement of his or her own position on an issue. You might even have to deal with someone erroneously reinterpreting your message for the audience.

What steps can you take to maintain control and disarm a potentially damaging detractor? Most importantly, don't lose your temper. Don't even allow yourself to sound a little bit irritated. No matter how rude or obnoxious the questioner is, you must remain polite and not engage this person in a debate.

Imagine the following scenario:

The president of the school board is addressing a public meeting about plans to improve the honors-level offerings in the school. While most of the audience—primarily parents and teachers—is in agreement with the plan, there are a vocal few who oppose the plan because it will mean the hiring of three new teachers and the retraining of several others at substantial cost.

Mr. Brown, a frequently hostile member of the audience, asks the school board president a question based on faulty logic: "Why do the kids need these fancy honors courses anyway? They didn't have them when my kids went here and they're doing just fine now. The cost is going to put us older residents in the poorhouse." A few of Mr. Brown's supporters agree loudly and glare at the president.

The school board members are worried about public reaction because most of them are up for re-election and they know that there are a lot of Mr. Brown types among the town's voters. They also know that Mr. Brown has more money than Ross Perot and just can't stand the idea of parting with any of it. So it's important that the board's president diffuse the objection without giving the opposition a platform to discuss their position.

Looking directly at Mr. Brown, he replies, "Mr. Brown, what's truly at issue here is the ability of our students to compete for jobs and for college placement. As I said during our presentation, our current program is no longer providing students with the courses they need to remain competitive. What we are proposing will put our school back on track."

Then the school board president looks to another audience member for a question. If he has prepared carefully in advance, he will know which audience member will have a question that will reinforce, rather than detract from, his message.

If Mr. Brown persists, the president might say, "Mr. Brown, I'd like to talk to you about what we are doing to improve our educational program here. Perhaps we could take a few minutes to discuss your personal concerns after the meeting." Then he should go on to the next topic or question.

Thus, the school board president is able to repeat his key message while deflating the importance of the detractor's words (by giving them back to him). If he had said, "I don't agree with you that these programs aren't necessary" or "The cost of the new programs will be worth it because our kids need the programs," he would have been repeating Mr. Brown's sentiments. In addition, he manages to completely ignore Mr. Brown's inflammatory remarks about the poorhouse.

Another difficult situation for a presenter is the know-it-all who asks questions prefaced by a long-winded preamble. Such a person enjoys the sound of her own voice. Back at the school board meeting, you'll find this difficult audience member saying, "Well, you know, it's kind of interesting to note that for the past several years, and I've been here for twenty-five years now so I should know, we've been talking about ways to improve the educational system; and then, of course, there is always the issue of how much more taxes people can afford, especially people on fixed incomes like me. One the one hand, you have to think about the children . . . and on the other hand, there are the taxpayers to worry about; and you never know if you're getting it right . . ." She could, and will, happily go on all night.

This kind of audience member is actually a passive-aggressive person who may be purposely detracting from the speaker's key points with seemingly pointless droning. In this situation, you must reclaim control of the presentation by cutting the questioner off. Just do it politely with a smile on your face. At the point during her ramblings when she says, "We've been talking about ways to improve the educational system . . ." you say something like "And improving the educational system, Mrs. Peck, is exactly what we intend to do. As I pointed out a few minutes ago, with the three steps we've proposed, our district will be moving ahead."

Once Mrs. Peck has been acknowledged, you turn your attention to the rest of the audience, finishing with a nod to a different questioner. You are back in control.

Some long-winded types may have a legitimate question that does in fact pertain to your presentation. The questioner just seems to be having trouble getting it out. You can help that person articulate his or her concern and still retain control by summarizing the question so that it fits your point. Here's how: "What I understand your point to be, Mr. Sharp, is that in order for the new program to work well, the teachers will need sufficient time to train. And you're absolutely right. That's why a professional development segment of the program has been built into the proposal."

There are times when the same few questions seem to be repeated over and over. When this happens, it's time for the presenter to take charge of the situation and end the question-and-answer session by making a friendly glance around the room, folding up her notes, and saying, "How about one more question." This is a good opportunity to tie the question to your key point, thank the audience, and take your leave.

When you don't want to answer questions—perhaps because you know that your audience is decidedly hostile, or that you aren't likely to get appropriate questions, or that you have run out of time and must leave—be gracious, but firm. Look around the room, making friendly eye contact with as many leaders as you can identify, pack your notes, and say, for example, "I appreciate having the time to share the nuances of Project 21st Century with you. And I hope you'll take a few minutes to read the handouts. I'm confident they will further clarify the points we've covered today. Thank you." Then walk away from the podium and shake hands with your host.

In truly vicious situations—which are extremely rare—you are not under any obligation to respond. If you are verbally attacked, especially if the attack is personal in nature, you have every right to say you think that such a question or statement is inappropriate.

You might even say, "So that others can hear what I am saying, it might be best if you were to leave, sir." This is a situation where your assistant, or "second," could then escort the heckler out of the room. (See Chapter 6 on logistics for more information on assigning a "second.") Remember, this kind of situation is very unlikely to happen to you unless your topic is uncommonly controversial.

Other difficult situations occur when an audience member uses accusations, hypothetical questions, inaccurate statements, "Do you still beat your wife?" questions, or downright hostility. You can remain in control and, if not come away completely unscathed, at least retreat gracefully with minimal damage if you follow these rules:

- Never lose your temper.
- Don't resort to name calling or accusations.
- Remain calm.
- Always tell the truth.
- If you don't know the answer to a question, say so. Then offer to find out the answer or offer a source for finding the answer.
- Don't pursue "What if?" questions unless you feel comfortable doing so.
- Don't answer hypothetical questions. Instead say, "That's a hypothetical situation. Let's look at the reality," or something to that effect.
- Feel free to say, "I don't agree with your point of view, and this is why."
- Look for areas of agreement within a disputed point to lessen someone's argument. Try a "minus-plus" phrase like "While we will experience some belt tightening in the initial stages of the program, we expect the final outcomes to strengthen our position within a year."
- Never repeat someone's negative point of view in your answer to a question.

It may help to have a few stock phrases or sentences in your arsenal of responses to use when things get a little rough. Here are some that might be worth committing to memory:

- "That's not a position we've looked at before. Perhaps we can explore it at the next meeting."
- "Tonight we need to stick with the agenda" or "We don't have time to stray from our agenda tonight."
- "Though that's a valid issue, today we are here to talk about . . ."
- "Let's get some questions from those who haven't had a chance to speak yet." (This is useful when you need to cut off the pest who has too many insignificant questions.)
- "I'm not sure I see the connection with the topic we're discussing now. Why don't we save that for later."
- "I don't know the answer to that question. If you'll leave your card with my assistant, I'll send you some background information next week." (If you use this line, you must be prepared to follow through with your promise!)
- "I'm afraid we have time for only one more question."
- "Actually, that's not within my area of expertise. You may want to consult with . . ."
- "There may be some truth to that point, but the fact remains . . ."
- "Have I answered your question?"
- "Unfortunately that issue is really too complex to discuss here."

I hope you'll never experience an audience that's so hostile they get up and walk out en masse. But that's exactly what happened to the CEO of a pharmaceutical company. Hours before his scheduled talk to investors, a newspaper article was published that stated that the CEO's company had just won FDA approval for a new and extremely innovative drug, and it was about to be launched on the market. The investors were ecstatic because they were now going to see some return on their very large investments. But the CEO had to stand up and tell the group that the reporter was misinformed and that the drug, though successful in clinical trials, was still many months away from the marketplace. The audience was incensed and stormed out while the poor CEO stood at the podium.

He has survived. His company is doing well, that drug and several more have won approval from the FDA, and the investors are making lots of money. But I wouldn't be surprised if the recollection of that moment can still make him sweat.

Three

The Presentation: Put It All Together

The mode by which the inevitable is reached is effort.

—FELIX FRANKFURTER
ASSOCIATE JUSTICE, U.S. SUPREME COURT

Because you are reading this book, we'll assume that you are about to make a presentation. This chapter looks at the best way to prepare, to position, and to present your message to your prospective audience.

Before you start to prepare your presentation, identify its purpose and define your goals, using the categories defined in Chapter 1. And you must define your audience, using the strategies discussed in Chapter 2. Then, by asking yourself the following questions, you'll be able to structure your presentation to meet the goals you have set:

- What does my audience expect to gain from this presentation?
- What do they already know about the topic?
- Do I expect this presentation to persuade, inform, entertain, or a combination of these?
- What are my key points?
- What one thing do I want them to remember most?

- What materials do I need to prepare and to deliver my presentation?
- What delivery format will I use?
- What kind of assistance can I expect to have?

But first there are a few basics that may help you create a presentation you'll be proud of.

ACCORDING TO ARISTOTLE

> *A speech has two parts. You must state your*
> *case, and you must prove it.*

> —ARISTOTLE
> *RHETORIC*

Just as artists must learn the basics of drawing and painting before developing their own styles and musicians need to understand music theory before making interpretations of other's work, those who stand up in front of a crowd and deliver a presentation or speech will be well served if they have a good grasp of how a classic speech is composed. It may be academic, but it's worthwhile knowing.

When Aristotle wrote the words in the preceding quote, he was referring to persuasive speeches—those talks that are designed to change or form attitudes and opinions, to build consensus, and to foster understanding. He taught that persuasive speeches included a statement that defined the thought, and an argument that got that thought across to the audience.

But Aristotle also said that those two parts made up the most basic kind of persuasive speech, and that most speeches were made of four parts:

- Introduction
- Statement

- Argument
- Epilogue

Of course, not all speeches are designed to be persuasive. Wilbur Howell, the author of the speech handbook described in Chapter 1, explains in his text that "speeches are admirably suited to the transfer of understanding from one person to a large group in a single operation. By one oral 'publication' the learning a man has acquired can become the property of men, with no expense involved in transmission." Though Mr. Howell would raise a howl from even moderate feminists today with his biased language, his description of an expository speech is succinct and on target.

Cicero, another great Greek orator, wrote that speech-making was made up of six different parts:

- Introduction
- Narration
- Division
- Proof
- Refutation
- Conclusion

Wilbur Howell was more in favor of Aristotle's simpler, four-part speech formation and further simplified it with a little descriptive language. Following Aristotle's teaching, he suggested this format for an expository speech:

- **Introduction**
  This part of the speech "seeks to get the speaker's subject before the audience in an interesting and significant fashion." This is the part where you tell 'em what you're going to tell 'em. (We'll look at this concept later in this chapter.)

- **Central theme**
  Here the speaker "seeks to characterize the subject as a whole so that its parts or aspects are indicated." I think Mr. Howell was trying to say that this is the part where you tell 'em.
- **Discussion**
  This is where you "take up each part or aspect in turn and elaborate each until the audience has the desired understanding of it." In other words, tell 'em some more.
- **Conclusion**
  Finally, the speaker "takes leave of the subject by summarizing what has been said, or by offering comments of supplementary interest about aspects of it not previously stressed by the speaker." Translation: Tell 'em what you told 'em. And then have a Q&A session.

Again referring to Aristotle, a persuasive speech would follow these guidelines:

- **Introduction.** (This is the same as an expository speech.)
- **Central theme.** (Here is the speaker's proposition or point of view. Aristotle called it "the statement of case.")
- **Discussion.** (This is "an examination, one by one, of the speaker's reasons for believing in his proposition, each of these reasons being supported by facts and evidence.")
- **Conclusion.** (This is the same as an expository speech.)

Although I have been a bit flippant in dealing with this academic approach to public speaking, I don't for a minute devalue it. If you can internalize the concept of incorporating these four sections of a speech, and then find your own voice in expressing them, you will be well on your way to preparing a winning presentation.

THE FORMAT

Speech preparation may be defined as the process of making decisions beforehand upon the content, the organization, the wording, and the delivery of a speech.

—WILBUR S. HOWELL

Once the date has been set and the audience defined (see Chapter 2), at least in the broadest terms (who and how many), you'll want to settle on a format for your presentation. Among the factors that will affect your decisions are the logistical considerations, for example, the venue, seating arrangements, and costs. (Many of these details are covered in Chapter 6.)

The logistical aspects of your format may be completely obvious. For example, if your presentation is a talk to a very large group, the physical format will likely be theater style in an auditorium or large hall, with you, the speaker, up front on a stage or at least at a podium. Training sessions are often presented in a classroom format; sales presentations can be one-on-one formats in a restaurant or office, or full-blown multimedia events in the company conference room.

The logistical format of your presentation will also depend on the level of audience participation or hands-on activities you have in mind, the types of visuals you'll use to support your presentation, the number of people who will attend, your budget restrictions, and the ambiance you want to create. In regard to ambiance, which is the atmosphere, character, or feel of your presentation, a lot will depend on the venue and the seating arrangements (see Chapter 6), and your tone and delivery style (see Chapter 4).

In addition to logistical and delivery considerations, you will need to address content format planning, which includes what you will say and how you will actually present your material. Here again, the format you select will depend on what it is you want your presentation to accomplish—whether your goal is to inform, to persuade, or to build goodwill, or some combination of these goals. Whatever format you choose, always remember who your audience is and never forget the "What's in it for me?" factor.

WHAT'S IT ALL ABOUT?

It's time to settle in and plan what you're actually going to say.

You need to know the purpose of the presentation and understand what it is you want to accomplish before you can actually do the research, make an outline, gather your slides, prepare your handouts, and write the words you will say. Sometimes it helps to give your presentation a title. At other times this will have been done for you. And on a few occasions, a title will spring from your head in the middle of the night—be sure to get up and write it down, or you'll probably forget a perfect gem.

By putting a name to what you plan to say, you can set some kind of parameters around, or at least an umbrella over, the topic, letting you zero in on your content. You may start out with a subject that's too broad, but by steadily narrowing the focus, as you would when you take a photograph with a zoom lens on your camera, you can make your subject clearer for both you and your audience.

Here's an example of narrowing down the subject. Say I've been asked to give a presentation to a group of horticulturists at an annual professional association meeting. My specialty is English gardens, but the actual presentation topic is up to me. My purpose is primarily to inform, but I also want to entertain. So I start out with *a sampler of English gardens*.

That's a bit broad—I could talk about thirty-five different gardens, but the audience is too knowledgeable for an overview. This isn't a travelogue, after all, but a presentation on gardens to gardeners. So I narrow the subject matter to *the gardens of Somerset*.

By focusing on about ten gardens in one county in the Southwest of England, I can concentrate on a specific climate, point out the similarities and differences among gardens within 20 miles of each other, and simply give more detail on each garden. But perhaps the audience is interested in really getting into some depth. After all, these are people who know gardening and garden design and want to find out about things they don't already know. I can zoom in even further, creating a presentation on *Gertrude Jekyll, Penelope Hobhouse, and Margery Fish— three great gardeners and their work in Somerset.*

Okay. So the title is a little long. I can polish that up a bit later. But I now have a subject that is highly defined and very specific. The audience will hear how three of England's well-known gardeners—one from the earliest part of the century, one from the 1930s and 40s, and the third still designing today—have created or restored some outstanding gardens in one small part of England. Now, if the audience is a particularly well-informed group, they may get even more enthused about a talk with the title *Hestercombe—Gertrude Jekyll and Edwin Lutyens's masterpiece of garden design.*

By narrowing the focus to one garden, I can go into the fascinating details of one of the most beautiful and exciting garden designs I have ever seen. And the audience will go away with a wealth of information that they can use in their own garden design work.

Almost any subject can be refined with this approach. But there are times that it must be done in reverse. For example, your subject may start out as "Creating special events for new retail stores." That's a nice, narrow focus. But maybe it's too confined for your audience—the county chamber of commerce. By stepping back a little, you might broaden the subject to "Publicity and promotion for small businesses." That may be still a tad narrow, so by widening the view, you can create "Marketing made easy: Advertising, publicity, and promotion for small business."

With this new, broader title, you can cover a lot of ground and reach people at different levels of experience. During a Q&A session, you might explore a few better-defined subjects, or you might open the door to a series of increasingly specific presentations as the audience becomes more familiar with the subject.

ORGANIZE YOUR THOUGHTS

Once you have defined your topic, completed your research, and determined a format, you'll need to organize the material so that it conforms to your purpose. Kitty O. Locker, an expert on business and administrative communication, suggests following one of five standard organizational formats.

One way to organize your presentation is to work chronologically—for example, from the past to the present looking to the future. Once you have your thoughts organized, you can move the sequence around to, say, the present back to the past back to the present and on to the future. Your presentation would state how things are now, look to the past for reasons why things are as they are, reassert how things are, and project how things will be.

A problem-solving approach to the organization of a presentation begins with the problem, explores causes, and then provides a solution. Ms. Locker points out that this organizational format seems to be most effective with an audience that is likely to accept your solution.

When audiences are not as willing to accept your solution to a problem, you may want to use an organizational format that excludes alternatives. In this structure, you identify the problem and explain the symptoms. Then, one by one, you identify solutions and show why they are faulty. Finally, you present your solution and explain why it is the one that will work.

With a pro/con pattern, the presenter lists all the positive aspects of a situation or solution, and then gives the negatives.

This is particularly effective when the audience is in favor of what you consider the negative side, because it gives you the opportunity to show them why they are wrong.

And finally, there is the 1-2-3, or ABC, approach to organizing your presentation. As you'll see later in this chapter, people tend to remember things that are presented in groups of three. In this presentation format, you offer your topic in such a grouping. For example, you might say, "Today we'll look at marketing communications in terms of publicity, promotion, and packaging."

KNOW YOUR MATERIAL

So, you've been asked to (or maybe you're simply expected to) make a presentation. Chances are it's on a subject you already know an awful lot about. You're probably an expert. Why else would they ask you, after all? But even experts need to bone up on their topic before standing before a group and making a presentation.

Do you have all the facts and figures? Is your information up to date? Have there been some recent developments or changes that are a little sketchy in your mind? Do you have a firm grasp on the chronology of your topic? What happened before you joined the team? You may need to do some research!

There are presenters who have all the information at their fingertips because they live and breathe their topic. This is their baby, the research project they've been developing for the past twenty years, the book they spent five years writing, the thing they love most in life. These presenters won't have the dilemma of not having all the relevant data. Instead they will more likely need to figure out how to narrow or broaden the focus so the presentation is appropriate for the audience.

Then there are folks who give the same presentations, or various versions of it, dozens of times a year, or even once a week, so their biggest problem isn't knowing their material, but finding ways to make it sound fresh and interesting after the hundredth telling.

Let's say I'm going to make a presentation on the gardens at Hestercombe, with a focus on the design. Although I've visited the garden, have taken plenty of photographs, and have a solid understanding of the design concepts used there, I still need to do some research to fill in a few gaps.

To prepare for the presentation, I will review my slides and probably take notes on the details I find there. Next, I will go over all the printed materials I have on the garden and the designers, again taking notes.

By reviewing the notes, I'll see some repeated themes, patterns, and motifs that will help me establish a few key points. Finally, I'll go to the library and look for references to the garden and its designers, including a search through periodicals.

Once I've finished the research, I'll have far more information than I could possibly use in a forty-five-minute presentation. So I might want to create a mind map (see the following section) to help me establish what to keep and what to exclude.

PREP TIME

It takes three weeks to prepare a good ad-lib speech.

—MARK TWAIN

As you can see from the process I've outlined in the preceding sections, planning a presentation, even about a subject that's well known to you, is a time-consuming process. But it's difficult to say exactly how much time you should spend in preparation.

The Reverend David Anderson, an Episcopal priest, says he usually spends about ten hours each week to prepare his twelve- to fifteen-minute Sunday morning sermon. That would translate to about thirty hours of preparation for a forty-five-minute talk, a fairly standard length for a presentation. David Fredrickson, a

Presbyterian seminarian I spoke with, told me that in his recent training, twenty hours of prep time for a twenty-minute sermon was deemed appropriate.

Terry C. Smith, in *Making Successful Presentations—A Self-Teaching Guide*, agrees with the Presbyterians that you should devote *at least* one hour for every one minute of your presentation. Of course, it's not always possible to give that much time. After all, you also have the rest of your job responsibilities, a family to think about, or maybe even a little bit of a life.

But it almost goes without saying that the more time you spend in preparing and practicing your presentation, the more likely you are to succeed. In most situations, you won't be asked to give a major presentation without plenty of advance notice. If you have a month to prepare, you could spend an hour or so a day on your presentation, perhaps making your mind map while you're waiting at your daughter's soccer practice, reading a few periodicals on the train, or making notes for your slides during TV commercials.

When you truly don't have adequate time, you may have to beg off the invitation to speak and arrange for another date. If the invitation is actually a command performance and the date is not negotiable, you may have to drop everything and get to work, pull a few all-nighters, or assemble a team of assistants. The point is, in order to give a good presentation, you have to prepare thoroughly.

There are many instances—in business meetings as well as in civic, community service, or philanthropic settings—when you may be asked to make an impromptu presentation on a subject you are a known expert in. This specialized type of presentation situation is discussed in Chapter 9.

OUTLINE YOUR PRESENTATION

Most of us learned how to prepare an outline by about fifth or sixth grade. You start with Roman numeral headings, narrow the items down to capital-letter subheadings, and then create sub-headings after the numerals 1, 2, 3, etc. Finally, you list the details after lower-case letter headings. Outlines for presentations work the same way. It's pretty simple.

Wilbur Howell devotes Chapter II in *The Speaker's Abstract* to a discussion on creating an outline for an extemporaneous speech, and his advice is timeless. Here are his "Rules for the Outline" (they may remind you of your sixth-grade teacher!):

1. An outline is written in complete sentences, although the speaker, when delivering his speech, may reduce these sentences to notes in the form of words or phrases to jog his memory.
2. There is a sentence in the outline to control the development of each main part of the speaker's subject.
3. As has been indicated, the sentences are arranged under the following four headings:
   - Introduction
   - Central theme
   - Discussion
   - Conclusion
4. The main sentences under "Discussion" are given Roman numerals.
5. Subordinate sentences under "Discussion" or elsewhere are indented and given capital letters; and if more than one degree of subordination is desired, the sub-subordinates, so to speak, are still further indented and given Arabic numerals.
6. At the end of the outline, the speaker puts the title he or she wants the chair to announce in the introduction.
7. Additionally, at the end of the outline, the speaker lists things he or she has read in preparing his speech, or things he or she recommended the audience read, in case they ask for references to supplementary information.

Preparing an outline will help you focus on what you want to say, the order in which you want to say it, and the level of detail you want to use. Though Mr. Howell suggests using full sentences, few people actually do, and in fact, it's probably not necessary unless you are extremely insecure about your ability to present your subject.

Use the basic outline format, but by all means, use your key words and phrases instead of full sentences. How long should the outline be? Mr. Howell suggested that an outline contain from one-sixth to one-third the words of the speech to be presented. That means that, given the average of 120 words spoken per minute, an outline for a forty-five-minute presentation would have as many as 1,800 words. To give you an idea of how long that is, this paragraph contains eighty-seven words.

Although Mr. Howell's organizational advice is top drawer, we tend to work in a more streamlined manner nowadays. A detailed and useful outline can be arranged as a series of phrases or short sentences that give you the building blocks you need to construct your presentation. It should contain plenty of specific examples including the descriptive language you want to use when you actually present.

Your outline could look something like this:

Publicity for Nonprofit Organization Special Events (need catchy title)

- Tents are ordered, bands and clown are booked, pony ride is scheduled; but without adequate publicity, where are the crowds at your country fair?
- Where to start: Identify target audiences
  Mass media, geographic areas
  Internal audiences—staff, families, friends, members—use newsletters
  Others—vendors and suppliers, potential members, former members; who else?

- Media
  Press releases to newspapers—local tie-in for weeklies. Any celebrities?—handout sample press releases; calendar listings
  - One month prior
  - Three weeks prior
  - Two weeks prior
  - One week prior
    Magazines need six-month lead time—calendar listing
    TV—phone calls often aren't welcomed. Fax media advisory.
- Who, What, Where format (handout)—assignment editors. Celebrity tie-in?
    Radio—often overlooked but valuable resource. Ticket giveaways (sample letter to community service director)
    Public service announcements (samples)
    Newsletters, bulletins
- Posters, flyers
    Keep it simple, white space
    Distribution—someone you can trust with a crucial job
- Other ways to spread the word
    Banners
    Hot-air balloon
    Billboards and transit signs
- Working with a professional
    What a public relations consultant can do for you
    Fees to expect

A good outline for a presentation is as long as you think it should be. When you think you have everything covered, it's done.

CREATE A MIND MAP

Rather than taking the linear approach of an outline or list, you might want to try creating a mind map in order to develop your presentation. Kay Holmes, a veteran presenter and specialist in training sales, says this method allows you to make associations and connections among your ideas, thoughts, concepts, and abstract notions, and to organize your presentation according to these associations rather than in a strictly linear manner.

When it is completed, a mind map will look a little like a map you might draw on the back of a napkin when you're giving directions to a country house located in the middle of nowhere. All along the way are signposts and landmarks. Some people's mind maps look more like slightly quirky spider webs. In either case, a mind map lets you add information to your presentation without risking too much digression.

Here's how you do it.

Start with a central circle or box representing your presentation. Next, draw radiating lines that show the various aspects that must be dealt with, including subject matter, makeup of the audience, visuals, objectives, venue, logistics, travel considerations, and any other major piece of the presentation puzzle. Add these lines as you think of them.

From the radiating lines, add smaller lines (like side streets). These lines represent details and elements that are associated with the larger thoughts. Some of these smaller lines may result in dead-ends, whereas others may find links with previous lines. The process is much like a single-handed brainstorming session, and it works best if you write down everything you think of even if it doesn't make any immediate sense. Later in the process, as you analyze the map, it will become increasingly clear what things are relevant to your presentation and what can be thrown away. At this point you can cross out the irrelevant notes and add more details that fit.

Finally, you can redo the mind map clearly and legibly. You should wind up with a clear sense of direction and purpose and be ready to proceed to the next step in preparing your presentation.

You may find that working with colored pens or markers will help you define distinct themes for further development. Try using dotted lines and arrows to indicate different levels of connectedness. And sometimes it helps to use symbols or small drawings to further define your thoughts.

TELL 'EM WHAT YOU'RE GONNA TELL 'EM . . .

You've probably heard the following three sentences before. Though simplistic, they offer great advice.

- Tell your audience what you're going to tell them.
- Tell them.
- Then tell them what you told them.

Adhering to this little bromide—which is really a streamlined version of Aristotle's ideas on giving speeches—will keep you on track as you prepare your presentation. It will make your audience comfortable and secure because they'll know where you're headed. And it'll help keep you focused as you make your presentation.

The Opener

The first few words you utter will set the tone for your entire presentation. This is the part where you "tell 'em what you're gonna tell 'em." So it's imperative that you say something that will capture your audience's attention and give you rapport with the people. (Building rapport is covered in some detail in Chapter 4.)

There a number of ways to begin your presentation. You might start simply with a greeting: "Good morning. Thank you for inviting me to spend a few minutes with you today to discuss how we might work together to improve the quality of life for our less fortunate neighbors."

Then there's the shocker: "Thousands of teenagers die from drug overdoses every year. And this year, your child might be one of them."

You might introduce a little humor, but not of the "Did you hear the one about the priest, the minister, and the rabbi . . . ?" variety. Humor, which is discussed in detail in Chapter 4, is, by far, the most difficult way to open your talk. Only use it when you are absolutely sure that it's appropriate, that your delivery is impeccable, and that it's actually funny.

Instead of humor, you might choose a warm and friendly approach that could include an anecdote that lets your audience see you as human and credible. For example, "My mother was fond of clichés and she used them liberally. 'A stitch in time saves nine.' 'Moss never grows on a rolling stone.' 'A watched pot never boils.' She always had a cliché ready to help her family deal with life's situations. One of Mom's favorites was 'Never a borrower or a lender be.' Our organization needs to heed my mother's advice, ladies and gentlemen. I'm here this morning to tell you that under no circumstances are we in a position to borrow funds to support our campaign."

In this approach, the speaker has taken his mother's homely advice; and because we all have mothers, most of whom were capable of giving us reasonable advice at least some of the time, he has made himself one of the group. He has injected his personality, a little bit of himself, into the presentation.

If you are good with words, you could create some verbal imagery—that is, paint a picture with words so that your audience can *see*, not just hear, what it is you are saying. This takes considerable skill, but if it's something you can do, it's extraordinarily effective.

Other formats for opening your presentation include:

- An appropriate quote
- A short list of facts or figures
- A question
- A challenge or call to action

Whatever device you use to open your presentation, just be sure to "tell 'em what you're gonna tell 'em."

Chunk the Middle

A presentation has three major sections—the opener, the middle, and the close. The opener is the "tell 'em what you're gonna tell 'em" part. And the middle part, often called the body of the speech, is where you actually "tell 'em." This is where you get your message across, where you cover your key points, and where you "chunk" the bulk of your message. And there are a number of ways to do it.

Kitty O. Locker, of Ohio State University, suggests five different strategies for building presentations in general in her book *Business and Administrative Communication*:

1. Make a chronological progression from past to present to future.
2. Define the symptoms of a problem, identify the causes, and suggest or demonstrate a solution.
3. Explain the symptoms of the problem. Go through possible solutions. Then show how they don't work. Finally, give a solution that will work.
4. List all the pros of an idea, plan, or product. Then go through the cons, showing how they are outweighed by the pros.
5. Organize your presentation around three aspects of the subject. (See the following section, entitled "Speaking in Threes.")

In *Business Communication*, Gretchen N. Vik and Jeannette Wortman Gilsdorf write that informative presentations often include one or more of the following self-explanatory organizational elements:

Chronology	Cause and effect	Classification
Description	Narration	Problem and solution
Geographic	Illustration by example	Process
Compare and contrast		

You can choose one or two of these elements and organize your message within that context. Entertaining presentations use many, if not all, of the same elements that informative presentations do.

In *The Presentation Primer*, Robert Nelson and Jennifer Wallick go into great detail about making persuasive presentations, including details of Aristotle's classic "proposition and proof" approach to oratorical argument. They also cover the psychological progression model that first arouses interest, only to create dissatisfaction, and eventually works through the problem that causes dissatisfaction and finds solutions based on results and benefits. This is pretty complicated stuff.

It may be easier to think about the body of the presentation in a less academic way. You organize the presentation based on what you want to accomplish. In the case of a persuasive presentation, you can either define the problem, offer solutions, and identify the best solution or make a proposal (or state your thesis), build supporting arguments, create acceptance, and ask for action if appropriate.

Another approach to the persuasive argument—which, by the way, is the most difficult form of presentation and more likely to fail than informative or goodwill-building presentations—comes again from Vik and Gilsdorf. They point out that persuasion is often linked to motivation (you motivate your audience to act or accept).

To motivate an audience, presenters frequently follow a five-step process:

1. Grab the audience's attention with your opener.
2. Establish and build their need or interest in your product, idea, or proposal.
3. Show them that your plan, idea, or proposal will meet their needs.
4. Help the audience visualize, through descriptive language or with visuals, themselves using your product, idea, or proposal to meet their needs.
5. Encourage the audience to take the action you suggest.

Items 2, 3, and 4 form the middle of the presentation.

The editors of *The Executive's Guide to Successful Presentations* point out that most people are not capable of retaining more than seven key points. But even seven is a lot. Unless your audience is already well versed in your subject or highly motivated to hear what you have to say, it's probably best to limit your key points to three.

SPEAKING IN THREES

For some reason, the use of three points, examples, words, or ideas is more memorable than if you use just two or if you use four or more. It may have something to do with the sound or the rhythm of a series of three: healthy, wealthy, and wise; morning, noon, and night;

gold, frankincense, and myrrh; bell, book, and candle. You can probably add dozens to the list.

There may be some psychological reason as to why a series of three stays in our minds. But whatever the explanation, when you plan your presentation remember to use a series of three arguments, answers, or examples to make your point.

The Close

Finally, you're at the end of your presentation. You've made it through the whole thing. What do you say next? "Well, I guess that's it," is not one of the choices. There are presenters who actually do finish that way! No matter how eloquent you are for the opening and middle, if your close is a clunker, that's what the audience will remember.

So, go back to your purpose. What was your goal? If it was to inform, find out if you have given the audience the information it needs. This is the time to "tell 'em what you told 'em." You can accomplish this by saying, "I hope you now have a better understanding of what the marketing department has done to increase our market share in the sixty-five and over bracket. Is there anything you'd like me to clarify?"

If your presentation was designed to build goodwill and entertain, there may be no need to repeat your message or answer questions. Instead, you might just thank your audience and say good-bye: "Thank you for sharing your evening with me. I enjoyed our time together." It's often appropriate to thank your host and the audience: "I'd like to thank Ms. Hooper for inviting me to speak with you this afternoon, and to thank you all for making my visit so comfortable." It may even be appropriate to steal Red Skelton's famous "Good night and God bless."

When your presentation is of the persuasive variety, your closing is a little more important. You may want the listeners to take action, to accept your message, to buy your product, or to change their minds. In your closing remarks, you can do the following:

- Summarize your message.
- Repeat your key points.
- Ask for an action.
- Recreate the verbal imagery you used in your opener, but with the addition of your solution.
- If you began with an anecdote, end with another, but this time with a play on the words or some kind of memorable twist.
- End on a positive note, even when your message is a difficult one.

HIRE A SPEECHWRITER?

Eric Sauter has served as a speechwriter to the late Senator John Heinz and to a number of CEOs and top executives in the pharmaceutical and communications industries. And he has some very strong views about how the process should work. According to Sauter, far too often the speechwriter is separated from the person who will deliver the speech by levels of an approval process or layers of bureaucracy. Frequently, the speech must go through a half dozen or more reviews by people with varying standpoints or agendas.

Thus, the speech becomes watered down, mired in additions or deletions by people who have no skills in writing. When the speech is finally presented to the CEO or the senator, it bears only a vague similarity to the pithy, well-written thing it started out as.

Eric Sauter's advice for those who may find themselves calling on the services of a professional speechwriter is to work directly with the writer and to limit the number of others involved in the process. A good speechwriter will be able to glean what you want to say and will help you say it in a manner that reflects not only your thoughts but also your style and personality—essential elements to a successful presentation.

Four

Tone and Delivery: How to Engage the Audience

*The way to convince another is to state your
case moderately and accurately. Then scratch
your head, or shake it a little and say that is the
way it seems to you, but that of course you may
be mistaken about it; which causes your listener
to receive what you have to say, and as like as
not, turn about and try to convince you of it,
since you are in doubt. But if you go at him in a
tone of positiveness and arrogance, you only
make an opponent of him.*

—BENJAMIN FRANKLIN

How well you are able to reach your audience with a presentation
is directly related to two basic elements:

- What you have to say (see Chapter 3)
- The way you deliver what you have to say

In this chapter, we'll look at ways to build rapport with your audience and effectively deliver your message using humor, drama,
gestures, facial expression, and vocal variety. We'll also address
the issue of stage fright and offer a few techniques for minimizing its impact.

BUILD RAPPORT

To build rapport means to develop a relationship, especially one of mutual trust or emotional affinity. This sounds like a daunting task. We spend our lives working on our relationships with family, friends, and associates. Is it possible to establish a relationship with an audience, especially one filled with strangers, in the course of a half-hour talk or a half-day workshop? The answer is, of course, yes.

Naturally, the relationship you develop with a roomful of people won't be the same as it would be with a small group sitting around a restaurant table or with a one-on-one session with a prospective client. But it is possible to establish the kind of accord that leads to trust and affinity.

There's been significant interest recently in the concept of EQ—emotional intelligence. Individuals with a significant EQ are empathetic, intuitive, and perceptive, with a highly developed ability to put themselves in other people's shoes. Research on the subject shows that among people of equal intelligence, those with a well-established EQ are more likely to be high achievers because of their ability to predict other people's behavior and to understand their motivations.

While we are usually unable to increase our IQ, emotional intelligence can be learned. Daniel Goleman explores this fascinating subject in his book aptly titled *Emotional Intelligence*, and it's worthwhile reading.

By attempting to stand in another person's shoes, to see things through another person's eyes, any presenter can come closer to establishing rapport with another individual. Understanding the WIIFM (What's in it for me?) factor, at which we looked in Chapter 2, is a part of the larger task of building rapport.

One-On-One

You do it all the time. Every time you meet someone new at a cocktail party, on the tennis court, on the sidelines at your child's soccer game, or even in line at the grocery store, there is an opportunity to make a connection. All it takes is a genuine interest in getting to know the other person and to find something you have in common.

Say you have an appointment to meet a prospective client for an informal lunch. You've never met before, and all you know about this person is her name, her title, and the company she works for—not much to go on. But as we discussed in Chapter 2, by asking the right questions you'll begin to collect sufficient information to help you build rapport during your lunch.

The first thing you might do is to ask your prospect to pick the restaurant. This may give you a few clues as to tastes and interests. When you meet, do a quick inventory. Is she wearing a school ring? A wedding band? Is she dressed conservatively, or does she seem to be making a flashier fashion statement? Does she arrive breathless and rushed, or is she calm and organized?

Once you've gotten past the hand-shaking stage, jump right into the "get to know you" phase by asking appropriate questions. People generally like to talk about themselves, so it's usually not too hard to find out what makes them tick. Avoid saying things like "So tell me about yourself." Your prospect will be put off by such a broad request for information. Instead, ask how long she's been with the company or where she worked before joining the firm. Look for things you may have in common: sports, kids, hobbies, travel experiences, college, or a business background.

If there isn't much to go on, work on the here and now: Have you seen the new Spielberg movie? Do you have much experience with Thai food? Have you read the new book by so-and-so? How long have you lived in this city?

When your one-on-one companion gives you a few clues, follow up with questions: How did you get into growing orchids? What kind of equipment do you need to explore caves? Do you need much training to be a soccer coach?

During a preliminary one-on-one session, you may not get around to talking business, and often that's expected. By your next meeting, you should have developed enough rapport with your one-person audience to present your message in a way that will speak directly to him or her.

One-On-A-Table

A small group situation—say five to fifteen people—is like a small party. And, as the presenter, you are like a host. It's your job to put everyone at ease, to make them comfortable, and to keep the party moving along smoothly.

When the other members of the group don't know one another, be sure to make introductions, unless someone else is serving as host and you are one of the invitees. Five people are too few for wearing name tags, but you might want to consider it with ten or more.

You can begin to develop rapport with your small group by shaking hands with and giving a sincere greeting to each person. There won't be time to delve into each person's personal story, so instead your job is to fit the individuals into the whole. Where do they belong in the group? What is their role? You may have to hone your powers of observation to find out who is deferring to whom, where any hostilities may lie, and other dynamics of the group.

If possible, you should do some digging in advance, once you know who will be attending your small group presentation. This should be relatively easy if you are doing the organizing. If you're not, ask your host for some details about the rest of the audience. (See Chapter 2 for a list of questions to ask.)

A key to establishing rapport with this audience is to remember their names and to use them when addressing each person. That's easier said than done, but if you repeat each person's name when you are introduced, it will help you recall the name later. In some situations, it's appropriate to set up a seating chart and to mark each person's place with a name card or personalized handout packet. By retaining the master seating plan, and by making sure that each person sits in his or her assigned seat, you'll have all the names handy for easy reference, just in case you forget a name or two.

It's a good idea to arrive early for small group presentations. This will give you the necessary time to check the venue and any audiovisual equipment you may be using, as well as the opportunity to greet each person as he or she arrives, to be introduced if your host is present, or to introduce yourself if your host hasn't yet arrived.

While you may only have a few minutes, this extra time gives you a chance to make some kind of connection and to assess your audience members as individuals. When it's time to begin your presentation, you can take a minute to scan each face in the small group in order to make a personal connection.

One-On-A-Roomful

Larger groups require different rapport-building techniques. Humor (discussed later in this chapter) is one approach. Another avenue for building a connection with your audience is to ask *them* some questions. These questions should be relevant to your presentation.

When I present my slide talk on English gardens, I often ask for a show of hands with this question: "How many of you have visited gardens in England?" Then, of those who have raised their hands, I ask, "What garden there was your favorite?" Usually they mention one or two of the gardens I feature in my slides, and that enables me to lead into my talk with, for example, this statement: "This afternoon we'll visit some of your favorite gardens and some of mine." The very short interaction between my audience and me allows us to feel comfortable with each other and gets us ready to pursue the subject at hand.

When your goal is to pursue your audience to accept a new program, point of view, or plan, you might be able to establish rapport with them by involving them in the process and offering rewards or little gifts for good ideas. If your presentation is designed to inform, you can develop a rapport with your audience by asking them what they know about the subject.

One speaker I heard took a very esoteric subject—the spirituality of art—and involved her audience so energetically, she held them captive for thirty minutes. She began simply by asking people to name their favorite artists. A half a dozen people in the crowd of fifty were willing to call out the names of artists. Then she proceeded to explain the spirituality, or lack of it, in the work of these artists. And because her point of view was radically different from the perspectives of audience members, she continued to maintain contact with them by reacting to their reactions.

In order to establish a rapport with your audience, you must be willing to take a risk, to open yourself up to the people sitting in front of you, and to let your personality speak for you. There are a number of tricks experienced presenters use to break the ice with a large audience, including the following:

- Hand out raffle tickets to participants as they arrive, and award prizes to a half-dozen winners. Make the prizes relevant to your key points.
- Tape winning numbers to the bottoms of people's chairs.
- Ask for items from audience members' handbags or briefcases à la Monty Hall, and give out prizes.
- Ask people to tell you their expectations, and write them down.
- Hand out short questionnaires relevant to your topic, and have an assistant tabulate the answers. Refer to the questionnaires at the end of your talk.
- Ask for an assistant or assistants from the audience to help demonstrate a task

HUMOR

To place wit before good sense is to place the superfluous before the necessary.
—M. DE MONTLOSIER

Using humor in your presentation isn't always about telling jokes. It's about introducing amusing, whimsical, comical, or otherwise entertaining elements that make it easier for you to make a connection with your audience, to put you and them at ease, and to reinforce your message.

Presenters use humor at the start of their talks to loosen up the audience, to release tension, and to build rapport. By weaving humor through a presentation, the presenter helps his audience remain alert. And by linking an amusing anecdote or one-liner with a key point, he can add emphasis.

Some presenters use jokes to add humor, but this can be risky. Very few of us are born comedians. Professional entertainers whose stock in trade are funny jokes spend their lives perfecting their timing and delivery, and many fail. Even superstars like Don Rickles or David Letterman have had jokes fall flat. Because they are practically icons of the entertainment industry, Letterman and Rickles can afford the occasional bomb. You can't.

The other problem with jokes is that the humor in them is almost always at someone's expense. Can you risk the possibility of offending even one member of your audience with your joke?

A better way to add a little humor to your presentation is with funny stories, amusing quotes, anecdotes, or plays on words. If these things don't come to you naturally, seek them out. Try keeping a notebook of anecdotes. Clip cute stories from newspapers and magazines. I particularly like the Metro Diary column of the *New York Times* for its ironic and sometimes absurd twists on city life. *Reader's Digest* is another source of funny stories that aren't likely to offend anyone.

In your quest for usable humor, look for quotes by people such as Mark Twain or W. C. Fields. Some politicians have been particularly adept at incorporating humor in their deliveries. Ronald Reagan, for example, had an amazing talent for one-liners and amusing anecdotes, many of which are included in books about him. There are dozens of books of quotations on the market. Search for quotes that relate specifically to your message. If you can't find any, look for ways to twist them around a little so that they do.

> *Humor is emotional chaos remembered in tranquillity.*
>
> —JAMES THURBER

During my days with a major life insurance company, I would sometimes present the virtues of our national sports sponsorship program to the firm's agents. My audiences were most often entirely male, and many of these men were used to working with women who were only in subordinate positions. During those unenlightened times, women rarely worked through pregnancies.

I was seven months pregnant with my first child (and looking as if I were due any moment), and was scheduled to make a presentation to a group of agents in Rochester, New York. There were one or two women in the crowd, but the majority were men, and they looked a little uncomfortable about my condition.

After I was introduced, I took a minute to scan the audience. Then I smiled and said, "I spoke with my obstetrician this morning. He wanted me to assure you that I will definitely not have this baby today." They loved it and rewarded me with a big round of applause, lots of laughter, and understanding smiles. By using a little humor, I was able to address their obvious discomfort with having to deal with a hugely pregnant woman in a professional situation—a distraction that could have interfered with the success of my presentation.

A retired four-star general used the following story when be began his after-dinner address at a gala given by the Sons of the American Revolution. "When I first began to give speeches, my wife would tell me to make it interesting. Later, when I was more experienced, she would tell me to make it interesting but keep it short. Now that I'm at the pinnacle of my career, she tells me to pull in my gut." The general endeared himself to his audience with a quick,

funny, and self-deprecating story that just about everyone in the room could identify with. Brilliant!

DRAMA

Using drama to draw attention to key points or to create emphasis is a tool that takes considerable skill. In fact, it takes as much skill, or even more, to create a dramatic moment in a presentation as it does to add humor. And if you aren't careful, something you planned to be dramatic could become silly. But sometimes it's worth the risk.

Drama in a presentation isn't theater. Instead, it's a form of delivery that is serious, attention grabbing, and worthy of special note. It's a method of presenting your key point so that the audience isn't likely to forget it.

You can create drama with your timing, with your words, with your gestures, and with your voice. For example, if your presentation is about the AIDS epidemic in Africa, a dramatic delivery could include the following scenario:

You walk to the podium, and stand there for a full minute while scanning the audience. Then in a solemn, low-pitched voice you quietly say, "In the time it took me to walk from my chair to the podium, 350 people died of AIDS in Zaire. When we leave this room this afternoon, 7,500 more will have died." It's bold. It's heavy. And it's dramatic. The audience isn't likely to forget your message.

Numbers, ratios, and other cold, hard facts can help you add drama to your presentation. So will a smooth, slower-paced delivery. To add drama to your words, try creating one-word sentences to lead into your message. For a talk on teen pregnancies, a presenter might begin with this opening delivery: "Loneliness. Hopelessness. Anxiety. Anguish. Shame. These are things a teen mother lives with every day."

A dramatic delivery doesn't have to be downbeat, however. Take for example this opening delivery for a presentation on literacy training: "Hope. Freedom. Joy. This is what you can give to an illiterate man when you help him learn to read."

AUDIENCE PARTICIPATION

In the section on building rapport, we touched on the idea of involving the audience in your presentation in order to make a connection with the people to whom you are presenting. Audience participation, however, is useful for far more than breaking the ice. Other reasons to build activities for the audience to participate in include:

- To use up some of the stored energy people, especially children, have when they are seated for too long
- To wake people up, especially when your presentation is after a meal or the room is too warm
- To help the audience members master a task that you are training them to do
- To give the audience members hands-on experience with your product
- To emphasize a key point with an activity
- To answer questions

Stockbrokers frequently present financial planning seminars as an effective tool for building their client list. One particularly clever broker liked to enhance his rapport with the audience and to ensure their participation in the seminar by asking attendees to fill out blank index cards with their questions. His assistant collected the cards before the seminar began, and the stockbroker referred to them during his talk.

What most of the audience did not know was that the stockbroker had his own set of index cards with the questions he most wanted to answer—questions that emphasized and supported his key message points. By using a little trick, this speaker retained control of the seminar while making the audience feel that they had a hand in the direction of the talk.

STAGE FRIGHT

Fear is the darkroom where negatives are developed.

—ANONYMOUS

It's not all in your head! Stage fright is real, with undeniably physical symptoms—sweating palms and a nervous stomach in its milder form, soaking sweats and vomiting in more severe cases, and even total paralysis in its most debilitating manifestation.

If you are plagued by the fear of standing up in front of others, rest assured you are not alone. Many performers battle stage fright every time they approach the stage. The legendary Barbra Streisand was so consumed by stage fright that it actually prevented her from performing for years.

Much has been made of the psychological and physiological causes of stage fright and the animal instinct of "flight or fight" that make the hair stand up on the back of your neck, adrenaline race through your body, and your heart beat faster. But let's look at stage fright for what it truly is: the fear of the unknown in a situation over which you may have no control. It is indeed a natural instinct to be "scared to death." But, in fact, you will not die, even if your presentation is a total flop. When people are over-come with stage fright, they frantically ask themselves "what if" questions. What if the audience doesn't like me? What if I forget what I was going to say? What if I trip and fall on my way to the podium? What if the projector doesn't work?

Sure, some of those "what ifs" could possibly happen. But they most likely won't, especially if you are thoroughly prepared. The audience wants to like you. They expect you to succeed. After all, you are the expert who was invited to share what you know.

You won't forget your message if you have rehearsed enough. And anyway, you have your notes to help cue you if you have a temporary lapse. The projector won't fail because you checked it out just before show time. You aren't likely to trip, and if you do, so what? You'll catch yourself and go on. And the audience will admire your pluck.

Besides maintaining a positive, winning attitude, there are some tricks for overcoming or preventing a serious case of stage fright:

- Practice, practice, practice until you can give your pre-sentation in your sleep.
- Check and double-check your equipment.
- Breathe deeply but naturally. Hyperventilating may cause you to pass out.
- Loosen your muscles to release tension, especially in your neck and jaw.
- Take your time walking to the podium with your shoul-ders back and your chest and head up.
- Take a moment to scan your audience and focus on a few friendly faces. Smile.

If, after all your practice, your positive thinking, and your attention to detail, you find that fear is still getting the better of you, seek some professional counseling. You may be able to over-come your unreasonable fear with just a few sessions with a psy-chologist. A few people find taking a mild tranquilizer is the only way they can get through their presentations. However, if that's the case for you, it may be time to find another job.

READING YOUR SPEECH

There are occasions when reading words prepared in advance is the most appropriate delivery style for your presentation. Politicians and government officials often read prepared speeches or talks, as do the clergy, CEOs, and other top business officials. Lawyers and police spokespeople will read from a prepared text when they make official statements, and ordinary people sometimes are more comfortable reading a eulogy than attempting to speak extemporaneously.

Additionally, reading a speech is preferable to other forms of delivery when there is need for the audience to have exact information, legal issues are at stake, there is controversy, there is the potential for serious misunderstanding of the information presented, or you must, for whatever reason, deliver someone else's speech.

Most people don't like speeches that are read to them. That's because most people prefer a natural, conversational style of presentation. But there are ways to deliver a speech word for word that will sound more natural, be more interesting, and enable you to make a connection with the audience.

The best way is to use a Tele-Promp-Ter. This electronic equipment allows you to input your written speech and then have it displayed on a screen from which you then read. Tele-Promp-Ters are mounted on cameras in television studios to feed lines to newscasters and talk-show hosts. Good presenters always read and reread their material before airtime, because, even with the aid of a Tele-Promp-Ter, one should still know the material in advance.

If you won't have the advantage of a Tele-Promp-Ter, you'll need to read your prepared speech from pages placed on the podium in front of you. There are a few steps you can take to ensure a polished delivery:

- Prepare a final version of your speech incorporating all changes. If you make any last-minute changes, don't leave them scribbled in the margins. Have the speech retyped.
- Type the speech in capital letters and triple-space between lines. You may prefer to type the speech only half- or three-quarters of the way down the page to avoid having to lower your head to read to the bottom of the page.
- Instead of indenting paragraphs, try block paragraphing.
- Underline words or phrases you want to emphasize.
- Use a symbol you are comfortable with to note when slides or other visuals are to be presented. Be sure the person operating the equipment has the same notes.
- Read the speech aloud, and mark it for natural pauses.

You can devise your own marking methods. In *The How-To of Great Speaking*, Hal Persons recommends the following symbols for marking a prepared speech:

/	short pause
//	take a breath
X	end of thought
XX	long pause, look at audience
XXX	longer pause, take a breath, look at audience
<	raise your voice
>	lower your voice

DELIVERY DETAILS

- Keep your notes in a folder, or better yet a three-ring binder. This helps prevent the embarrassment of loose note cards flying across the stage.
- Type your notes with triple spacing on 8 ½" x 11" paper. Use an easy-to-read font, such as Helvetica, Palatino, or

Times Roman, in a bold format and a font size no smaller than 12 points.

- Place each page in a plastic sleeve that fits the binder. This makes turning pages easier.
- Walk to the podium confidently with your arms loosely at your side. If you are holding a folder with your notes, don't clutch it to your chest; hold it firmly in your hand with your arm at your side.
- Always stand tall. Relax your shoulders and pull them back. Hold your head high and your chin up.
- Smile naturally.
- When you arrive at the podium, pause. Take a breath, but avoid looking like you are gulping for air.
- Don't rest your elbows on the podium or lean on it. Stand with your weight evenly distributed on both feet.
- Establish eye contact with at least two or three members of the audience before you begin.

GESTURES

I should never have made my success in life if I had not bestowed upon the last thing I have undertaken the same attention and care I have bestowed upon the greatest.

—CHARLES DICKENS

Roger Ailes, who advised presidents such as Ronald Reagan and George Bush, writes in his book *You Are the Message*, "People who are the best communicators communicate with their whole being. They're animated, expressive, interesting to watch." How you move your arms and hands and the rest of your body during a presentation can have a big impact on your success as a presenter. Does that sound crazy? It really is true!

Think about the times when gestures seem to take on a life of their own. Comedian Dana Carvey made a name for himself imitating George Bush's stiff, choppy arm movements. And Norm MacDonald's *Saturday Night Live* portrayal of Bob Dole during the 1996 election played up the Senator's distinctive lack of gesturing (due to his damaged arm) to the point where his mannerisms became more memorable than his speeches.

To understand why gestures are such an important part of a presentation, spend a little time watching television. C-SPAN, the cable channel that broadcasts congressional activities along with other presentations and speeches in Washington, provides excellent role models, as well as some terrible presenters. Use what you see to perfect your presentation delivery.

Try watching C-SPAN speeches, news clips of speeches on CNN, or courtroom summations on Court TV with the sound turned off, and pay close attention to the speakers' gestures. Are there some that seem jerky and jarring, whereas others appear to be fluid and somehow comforting? Do some speakers use the same gesture over and over to the point where it is distracting to viewers? And how about a wooden speaker who barely appears to move?

Turn the sound back on and see how well speakers match their gestures with what they have to say. Does it look as if they are simply moving their hands for the sake of movement, or do the movements relate to the content of the speech, and reinforce the message with an emphatic hand movement?

Some speakers are remarkably creative in their ability to move their bodies in relation to the content of their presentations. Think about how you might support an idea or phrase with an appropriate gesture. If you aren't too inhibited, try acting out some of the following concepts in front of a mirror. Don't be afraid to exaggerate your movements.

- Unplug the life support for a terminally ill company.
- Pry open a closed mind.
- Circumvent a roadblock.

- Manipulate opinion.
- Nurture creativity.
- Guide a young person.
- Mold a generation.
- Breathe new life into a project.

This exercise is especially helpful for people who tend to stand stiffly erect and use gestures too sparingly.

If, on the other hand, you tend to move a little too freely or your gestures tend to be exaggerated, try making a speech with your hands clasped behind your back. Is it too hard to express yourself? Perhaps you'll need to work more on your content, vocal variety, and facial expressions and rely less on your hands and arms to get your point across.

For those who really aren't sure how they use gestures, it's time for a video check. Set your video camera on a tripod (or ask a friend, spouse, or child to help) and tape yourself reciting a short speech—anything really: a poem, the Gettysburg Address, the Lord's Prayer, or the message on the back of a cereal box. Try to be relaxed and natural and use the hand motions that you are most comfortable with. When you review the tape, you'll have an idea of how much work you need to do on your gestures.

While it's important to know how well you use gestures when you speak, you shouldn't use that knowledge to reinvent how you use your body. Instead, use what you know to *modify* your use of gestures in order to avoid looking like a robot or a whirling dervish.

Michael C. Thomsett, who wrote the *Little Black Book of Business Speaking*, warns against using *rehearsed* gestures because they look unnatural and unspontaneous, and can become distractions, especially when used repeatedly. So, if you feel uncomfortable with a gesture, chances are it's not appropriate for you or the situation. Leave it out of your presentation, and try to go with what comes naturally.

There are some gestures that are safer to use than others. Shaking a fist, pounding on a table, or pointing a finger are aggressive motions that rarely have a place in a business presentation. If you do plan to use these assertive moves, do so with caution and only when you need extraordinary emphasis.

When you make a presentation in another country or to a group from a culture other than your own, you'll need to pay close attention to your gestures to avoid the risk of offending your audience. For example, the A-OK hand signal (thumb and pointer finger forming an "O" with the other three fingers curled up above) is an obscene gesture in other parts of the world. The palm of the hand extended may mean "stop" to us, but for others it has rude connotations. Be sure to research the cultural idiosyncrasies of another country before you make a presentation there.

FACIAL EXPRESSION

> *If the world's a vale of tears, smile till rainbows*
> *span it!*
> —LUCY LARCOM

Roger Ailes points out that "facial expression is often the most difficult area of nonverbal communication to master because we are taught early that our faces can give us away. Many people, particularly business executives, freeze their faces regardless of the emotional state they are in. . . . But often you only gain complete credibility with an audience when they feel you're completely open and not masking anything from them. The viewer generally perceives the warmer, more vulnerable personality as being stronger and less afraid."

People react well to a sincere smile. It's almost as if they can't help it. A genuine, heart-felt smile is reassuring, soothing, friendly, and warm. It makes a positive impact. An insincere smile, on the other hand, is threatening and disturbing and will cause people to react negatively.

How well do you smile? Look through your old family photo albums for pictures of yourself. How do you look in most of them? Do you have a ready, easy smile, or are you the one in the group that always seems to have a serious look on your face? Or is your smile little more than a forced grimace?

If you are not a natural smiler, you need to do some work. Take a few minutes to try this exercise in front of a mirror when no one is around to inhibit you. First, try to completely relax your facial muscles. Start with your eyebrows and continue down your face to your jaw and neck muscles. Let your mouth hang open and your shoulders droop. Then think about something that really makes you happy. Try to imagine your feelings when you play with your grandchildren, run the dog on the beach, look at an especially beautiful person or scene, or see your child's soccer team win a big tournament. Let your face react to that happy thought. What happens? The corners of your mouth should turn up, and your eyes should narrow a bit. A real smile, one that is a result of happy thoughts, transforms a face because it shows real feelings. That's the smile you want to give your audience.

Is smiling always appropriate? Actually, it is. Even if you are bearing bad news, you can give your audience an understanding smile. Think about how we greet friends and relatives at a funeral. Though we are grieving, we still smile a greeting to people we care about. While our eyes will communicate our sadness, a smile is comforting and reassuring.

So when you must address a group about closing their neighborhood school, discontinuing a program, laying off employees, or other bad news, use a compassionate smile to soften the blow. One note of caution: Unless you're a terrific actor, if you don't feel compassionate, your smile will make you look like a phony.

A smile isn't the only effective tool in the realm of facial expression. I think there are few more potent looks than an exaggeratedly arched eyebrow. I have a friend who can raise one of her eyebrows in an arch so high it is worthy of Broadway. Just as a picture is worth a thousand words, so is a raised eyebrow! She can recite a list of objections or obstacles, then dismiss them without saying a word. In a second, opposition is reduced to rubble. If you have the gift of the eyebrow, use it.

VOCAL VARIETY

Variety's the very spice of life.
—WILLIAM COWPER

How well you use your voice is critical to the success of your delivery. In Chapter 8, we'll talk about improving the overall quality of your voice. But here, we'll discuss how to use variations in pitch and rate of speech.

The pitch of your voice is how high or low it is. Whereas a high-pitched voice is rarely, if ever, suitable for presentations, varying the voice from the middle range to a lower pitch is. Speech is effective in the middle range, with special emphasis possible by adding a lowered pitch to a very deep tone. Most women will not be able to speak in a low pitch, but they should strive to deepen a high-pitched voice. Men with very low-pitched voices may need to raise the pitch from time to time to avoid speaking in a monotone. A singsong approach, going from high to low pitch, is probably worse than a monotone and should be avoided.

Altering the speed of one's speech is another way to add vocal variety to your presentation. Though you shouldn't ever speed through your talk, speaking too slowly is a sure way to lull your audience to sleep. Use deliberate pauses, lasting about two or three seconds, to take a breath or to add emphasis. Coordinate a pause with a visual survey of your audience, taking the time to make eye contact. Pause for emphasis after making a key point. Wait a few beats before speaking after saying something dramatic.

E-NUN-CI-ATE

You may have a lovely, mellifluous speaking voice with a pleasing pitch and no problem adjusting the volume, but if you mumble or slur your words, no one will understand you. Few things are more annoying than a speaker who doesn't speak clearly.

To make sure that you enunciate your words clearly, use a tape recorder. Speak a few lines using your normal speech patterns and play them back. Can you distinguish the *s* and *f* or *b* and *d* sounds? Do words run together? You may need to work on your enunciation or articulation—that is, how you form the words using your lips, teeth, tongue, palate, and jaw. Consonant and vowel sounds are created when we use our teeth, lips, and so forth, and the muscles that control them, in different combinations.

In order to articulate clearly, you need to select the right combinations. If your articulation problems are severe, you may want to get professional help. But most people who mumble or slur will improve their articulation by paying more attention to the way they form words.

Slurred or mumbled words will eventually irritate an audience because they will have to strain to understand you. Poor articulation will also make you appear to be less believable and less authoritative. On the other hand, exaggerated enunciation will often make an audience feel that they are being patronized or spoken down to. You should strive to avoid both scenarios.

Five

Visuals

You've got to see it to believe it.

—ANONYMOUS

Did you know that most humans absorb more than 80 percent of what they learn through the sense of sight? That means if you *show* something to people, they are far more likely to remember it, at least for a while, than if you *tell* something to them. *Show* and *tell* at the same time, and your audience will remember even more.

Geri E. H. McArdle, PhD, who wrote *Delivering Effective Training Sessions* and has been a consultant to Fortune 500 companies, says that adding visuals such as graphs, charts, maps, or photos to a presentation increases the amount of retained information by as much as 55 percent. For example, people who have attended a show-and-tell presentation will retain about 65 percent of the information after three days, compared to about 10 percent retention for audiences who have simply heard the information.

A study done by the Wharton School of Business showed that the use of visuals reduced meeting times by as much as 28 percent. Another study found that audiences believe presenters who use visuals are more professional and credible than presenters who merely speak. And still other research indicates that meetings and presentations reinforced with visuals help participants reach decisions and consensus in less time. That's a pretty good case for using visuals!

WHEN TO USE VISUALS

A picture is worth a thousand words.
—CHINESE PROVERB

Nearly any kind of presentation will benefit from some form of visual aid. Shareholders will have a better grasp of earnings or losses when presented with pie charts or bar graphs to show them where the money went. Clients of an advertising agency will have a better understanding of what a new advertising campaign will look and sound like when they are presented with story boards for TV commercials and slides of magazine ads. New hires will catch on to customer relations policies through role-model performances on video. Gardeners will learn how to propagate plants from cuttings when they actually have the plant material in their hands. A prospective customer is more likely to understand your product, and feel the need to buy it, if he or she can see it or touch it. And a message such as "sell" or "service" or "quality" takes on greater meaning when it's projected on a screen or printed on a flip chart.

Sometimes visuals are essential components of a presentation. Examples of times when visuals are a "must" include the following:

- Your message is abstract, complex, or difficult to understand.
- Your key message or subject is visual in nature.
- It is essential that your audience retain your message.
- There is controversy or the chance your message could be misinterpreted.
- You have more than two or three key points.
- You want to add emphasis to a key point.
- The presentation includes words or language unfamiliar to the audience.
- The presentation is a how-to session involving several steps.

- You need to "dress up" a subject that may not be of great interest to the audience.
- The presentation includes numbers or mathematical calculations.
- You are dealing with children.

In the next section, we'll look at the various types of visuals and how to use them.

TYPES OF VISUALS
Visual aids take many forms, for example:

- Flip charts on easels
- Notebook flip charts
- Blackboards with chalk
- Whiteboards with markers
- Overhead transparencies
- Slides
- Videos
- Multimedia productions
- CD-ROM
- Computers
- Props
- Three-dimensional models
- Posters
- Banners
- Handouts

And there is enormous diversity for the potential content of your visual aids:

- Photographs
- Typography

- Graphics
- Lists
- Symbols
- Colors
- Shapes
- Charts
- Maps
- Graphs
- Diagrams
- Cartoons

Somewhere among all these possibilities and combinations will be the visual aid that will match your objectives, subject matter, delivery style, audience needs, expectations, and, very importantly, budget.

Slides

Slides are extremely versatile visual aids that allow the presenter to share photographic images, drawings, and other artwork, words, numbers, charts, graphs, and timelines with the audience. In the past slides were expensive and time consuming to produce. Today, computers and desktop publishing programs reduce the time and expense considerably.

In fact, a relative novice can now produce sophisticated slides using software programs like Corel's Presentation and Microsoft's PowerPoint for the PC, or Persuasion by Adobe for Macintosh. There are many more programs available, and new ones are being developed all the time.

The versatility and scope of slide design is as broad as any area of graphic art, and software packages offer exciting and attractive design options, though learning how to navigate your way through the program does take some time. Most community colleges offer extensive computer classes, including courses on graphic design. Even without training, using a little effort and the templates in the software, you can create attractive slides that incorporate interesting and readable typography, graphs, charts, maps, clip art, and other visuals.

If, however, you don't have the time or the inclination to learn how to use the design software, or if you think your sense of design is not as developed as it should be, hire a pro. You'll save time, and in all likelihood wind up with a better result. Advertising and public relations firms regularly perform this service for their clients. You can check with your local chamber of commerce for a list of graphic design studios. Print shops frequently offer slide-making capabilities too. Or you can look in the Yellow Pages under "Graphic Designers."

There are presentations that would be nothing without slides. Picture a talk about the endangered species of the Amazon jungle without slides of fascinating animals. Imagine a lecture about the historic chateaux of France devoid of photos. In these instances, photos don't merely add emphasis or clarity—they are essential to the presentation.

When I give a half-hour lecture on English gardens, I usually show about one hundred slides because visiting a garden is primarily a visual experience. In this case, my slides are supported by a running narrative about the plants and the garden design.

When you create slides to support your presentation, think first about what you need them to do. In some cases, as in my garden lectures, it's pretty obvious—the slides do most of the "talking."

However, most business presentations don't rely as heavily on slides. Instead they will serve as a kind of frame or format or as punctuation points for your talk. In addition, they help you, the presenter, with visual cues, which is especially helpful for the novice or for a presenter plagued by stage fright.

Use your outline to determine the appropriate sequences for slides and their content. It's rarely appropriate to simply reproduce your outline. Instead, you should pull out key words and phrases, make short bullet point lists, and clarify key points or concepts with illustrations. Don't carry a sentence or a key point over to the next slide, and try to keep each point short.

Here are some tips for creating slides:

- Limit one "thought" per slide.
- Don't use more than five lines of type, five words per line, on each slide.
- Be consistent in how you use dark typography on a light background or light type on a dark background.
- Be wary of fancy type faces; they must be readable.
- Use type styles with a serif (the little "caps" and "feet" on letters) for the text and without serif for headlines and titles.
- Make sure the type is large enough so all audience members can read it.
- Don't overuse capital letters—it reduces the emphasis.
- Avoid a "busy" design.

Studies show that slides or other visuals that combine graphic images such as drawings, cartoons, photographs, or symbols with the typography are more effective than typography alone. Charts and graphs are also more interesting when they combine some interesting graphics. It bears repeating, "One picture is worth a thousand words."

Color is also essential. There has been extensive research, especially by advertisers, into the psychological impact of color. The *McGraw-Hill 36-Hour Course: Business Presentations* by Lani Arrendondo devotes more than two and a half pages to the nuances of color in visual aids, and some of the concepts are intriguing. For example, one finding showed that the use of color in advertising copy increased readership and retention by as much as 80 percent.

But the key to using color is *which* color. Apparently, men prefer and remember violet, dark blue, olive green, and yellow, in that order; women have the best recall when dark blue is used, followed by olive green, yellow, and red.

Lani Arrendondo also offers this color wisdom:

- Blue is the favorite color of most people.
- Earth tones such as dark orange and brown are associated with friendship.
- Red can mean either power and speed, or can evoke images of debt.
- Although black speaks with authority and strength, it is also associated with death.
- Violet makes people think of dignity, but is also conservative and frugal.
- Yellow seems to invoke confidence and optimism.

In addition, you should heed this advice:

- Keep your color palette limited to two or three per slide.
- Use bright colors for key points.
- Indicate minor points with lighter shades.
- Avoid using red and green together because people who are color blind will not be able to tell them apart. It also says "Christmas" to most people.
- Be consistent in the use of color for symbols or images that carry through your presentation.
- Use dark shades of blue, green, red or purple, and black for headlines, titles, and key words.

The following slides might be used for a simple presentation to a city council proposing the creation of a downtown historic district:

Slide 1: A graphic rendering of an antique building—two colors on a light blue background

Slides 2, 3, 4, and 5: A bullet list of short-term benefits (or a set of cumulative slides on which each new benefit is added to the one before on subsequent slides)—dark blue background, light blue type, yellow bullet points

Slide 6: Costs—green background, light type

Slides 7 and 8: A bullet list of long-term benefits—medium blue background, light blue type, yellow bullet points

Slide 9: Funding sources—green background, multicolored pie chart, yellow type

Slide 10: An action plan—graphic of a yellow checklist, light blue background, black type, red check mark

Slides 11 and 12: One or two summary slides—dark blue background, light blue type

Slide 13: House graphic—multicolor, light blue background

In all, this talk might include as few as eight slides or as many as thirteen or fifteen if the lists of short- and long-term benefits, funding sources, and action plan points were longer.

Some tips for working with slides include:

- Use a remote control device for advancing slides.
- If you don't have a remote control slide advancer, devise an unobtrusive signal for the person who will operate the projector.
- If you have a prepared script, mark it with slide cues and give a copy to your assistant. Be sure to go over the script with him or her in advance.
- Use a laser light pointer; wooden pointers look old-fashioned.
- Dim the lights, but don't turn them off completely.
- Be aware that projectors can make noise, so you may need to raise your voice.
- Place the projector high enough so that it isn't projecting upward toward the screen.
- Stand to the side of the screen, not in front of it.
- Look at the audience, not at the screen.
- If you must look at the screen, do not speak while facing away from the audience.
- Set up and test your equipment before the audience arrives.

- Before the audience arrives, make sure that the screen is visible from every seat.
- Allow "just in case" time for equipment problems.
- Turn the projector off and turn the lights up as soon as you have finished showing your slides.

Keep in mind that slide trays are not necessarily inter-changeable. I bought a used projector to use when I give slide lectures. The projector came with two carousels, but I soon found that I needed more trays when I reorganized slides for different audiences. The projector was made by an obscure manufacturer and didn't accommodate any other trays. Fortunately, I found a dozen used trays that were compatible with my projector, so I have enough for now. But when the projector wears out, the carousels will be obsolete and I'll have to replace them too.

It's important to know that your slide carousels will be compatible with the projector at the presentation venue. If in doubt, bring your own projector. And always have at least one spare projector bulb.

When pharmaceutical companies make presentations before the FDA, there is usually a lot at stake. So the company representatives want to be prepared for every possible question or circumstance.

Recently, representatives of one of the country's major pharmaceutical companies appeared before the FDA to win approval of a new over-the-counter heartburn remedy. The team that prepared the presentation had ordered more than 1,000 slides in order to cover any possible question that might be asked by the FDA officials. In the end, the team from the pharmaceutical firm used only fifty of the

slides, and their product was approved. A competitor went through the same process for a similar product. This competitor prepared a fraction of the number of slides, and also won approval.

Which company's approach was better? There's no way to know. The point is, if you can afford to make 950 extra slides, and it makes you feel better about your presentation, then do it. Just don't show them all!

Overhead Transparencies

Probably the most often used visuals for business presentations are overhead transparencies. These are the transparent sheets of acetate with words and graphics printed on them that are projected on a wall or screen via an overhead projector. In the old days, overheads almost always consisted of pages of type. But today, nearly anything you produce on a laser printer can be transferred to an overhead transparency.

Here again, presentation and graphics software can play a big role. You can incorporate color, artwork, and all kinds of graphic images to enliven your presentation. And transparencies have the advantage of allowing you to use a grease pencil during your presentation to circle a number, underline a word, or add an exclamation point. Another advantage is that the room doesn't need to be as dark as it does with most slides.

When using transparencies, plan to have a "staging" area on either side of the projector—one for upcoming sheets, the other for after the sheets have been presented. This can help eliminate that awkward moment when transparency sheets slide off the corner of the projector stand and flutter around the room. And remember, when transparencies are mounted in cardboard frames, they are easier to handle.

Keep in mind that it is distracting to look at a visual when it is not relevant to what is being said at a given moment. To avoid this situation, keep transparencies covered when you are not referring to them.

Some people like to slide a sheet of paper down a transparency, covering the images or words below until they get to that point. Using this practice reduces the number of transparency sheets you'll need; however, while it is an acceptable method, it is somewhat amateurish. It's more professional to have separate sheets.

If you have more than two or three minutes between transparencies, turn the projector off. They tend to make a lot of noise and to generate heat, which may be distracting, particularly for those seated nearby.

Video

We live in a time when television seems to dominate our lives. With cable, we have anywhere from 30 to 60 or 70 channels depending on where you live, and most of them have programming scheduled 24 hours a day. Video cameras are common household devices, and families everywhere are building video libraries. Some audiences, especially younger ones, *expect* the action and movement of television and video and might not be able to relate well to the pace of slides, overhead transparencies, or flip charts. Video, therefore, can be a valuable tool for some presentations.

Suppose you are leading a meeting about the impact of snowboarding on the ski industry. Wouldn't a three-minute video clip of snowboarders swooshing down a mountainside be a more compelling visual than three minutes of slides of the same activity? I think so.

Or imagine your topic is the needs of imprisoned teenage mothers. Don't you think a videotaped segment of a day in the life of such a young mother might make a stronger impact on your audience than slides or overhead transparencies? Of course it would.

The key to using video successfully is the quality of your production. Sure, anyone can use a video camera—ask any mom or dad who has visited Disney World. But a presentation video is different from your basic home movies.

Before you start on any kind of video production to support your presentation, work up a budget, decide on a length, develop an outline, and then prepare a story board. The story board resembles cartoon panels with drawings of each scene location, the people in the scene, a brief description of the action, and a bit of the dialogue.

Once you've developed a story board, look for professional assistance. You'll find video production houses in the Yellow Pages. Or you can consult with your professional association or chamber of commerce for recommendations. Ask for names from the film department of a local college or university, or call an advertising agency or a PR firm, some of which offer their own video production services. But don't hire anyone until you've seen some examples of his or her work.

Videos take time and money to produce, so this isn't something you should jump into without careful thought and planning. Be sure to allow plenty of time—you'll need several months at least—to find and hire a production house, write the script, shoot the video, edit it, and produce the final piece.

One of the wonderful advantages of video is that it can be adapted for other uses. For example, the snowboarding video could be lengthened to become a twenty-minute promotional piece and sent to ski clubs, ski equipment stores, and other organizations. Or it can be shortened to one minute and used as a commercial.

Multimedia

Sometimes a presentation needs to provide lots of razzle-dazzle. Trade show exhibits, national or regional sales meetings, and product introductions may require a touch of show biz in order to claim the audience's attention and persuade them to accept the message, or just to impress them in a big way. These occasions call for a multimedia presentation that could include the use of two, three, or even twenty slide projectors, voice-over and musical audio tracks, video stations, animation, CD-ROM, and hyperlinks to the Internet.

In the past, multimedia presentations—because they require technological sophistication along with the skills and talents of animators, actors, graphic specialists and recording studio staffers—were almost always planned and produced by professional studios or agencies. But today, according to Dave Roberts, a multimedia consultant, developments in software make multimedia production so easy, he knows a six-year-old who can do it. That must be some six-year-old! And most high schools offer courses or at least curriculum units on multimedia production.

Amateurs *can* effectively use the software to create graphics, animation, and even handouts for a presentation. They can record their own music or pay royalties for the use of recorded music and scan or create images using their own photos or artwork.

But not everyone can produce a masterful presentation. It will only be as good as your own skills, talent, and creativity. If you aren't really good at using the computer and this kind of software, hire someone to create the multimedia presentation for you, or consider a smaller scale presentation with other appropriate visual aids.

Always keep in mind that the multimedia show should enhance your message, not become the message. If the show is too showy, it becomes the main attraction rather than a support mechanism. So, while you plan your multimedia presentation, ask yourself these questions:

- Is there so much going on in this presentation that the key messages are being lost in the glitz and glitter?
- Are the graphic images relevant to the message?
- Is the expense of creating this presentation in proportion to the importance of the message?
- Can I manage the equipment myself?
- Do I have the staff to set up and run the equipment?

It is possible to transform an ordinary slide presentation into a multimedia production with the simple addition of music and/or sound effects. Usually the music and sound effects are selected first, followed by the preparation of a sound track. Then the slides are timed and cued to the music.

It's tricky for amateurs to prepare sound tracks themselves, and unless you are a musician and write and perform your own music, you'll run into the problem of obtaining permission to use other people's recordings. A sound studio will help you put a professionally recorded and edited sound track together, and the costs aren't necessarily prohibitive. You'll find these firms listed in the Yellow Pages of most city phone directories. You may also get recommendations from radio stations and advertising agencies. Or call a company whose radio advertising you admire, and ask them who prepared the sound track.

Flip Charts

Flip charts are low-tech visual aids that are usually easy and inexpensive to prepare. The basic format consists of essentially a large pad of blank paper attached to an easel stand. Smaller desktop or notebook types are often used for sales presentations (either a spiral-bound notebook for easy page turning or a ring binder, so pages may be added). Often desktop flip charts fold open like a portfolio and can also hold handouts or other materials.

Informal presentations take on a dynamic energy when the speaker develops key points by writing them on blank flip-chart pages. The energy is sustained when the pages are ripped from the chart and taped in sequence to the walls as the presenter builds his or her case. This is a very physical kind of presentation and requires a sustained level of activity on the part of the presenter. To avoid the distraction of flip-chart sheets falling off the walls, the presenter needs to devise a secure method of taping them up.

Often flip-chart pages are prepared in advance with key points, diagrams, charts, and calculations printed on them. Because it's important that the visuals relate specifically to the subject of that moment, experienced presenters leave a blank page between each printed page. This way, when one point is covered, the printed page can be turned, revealing a distraction-free blank page. Separating pages will also prevent the marker from bleeding through to the next message page.

Some speakers who don't trust their ability to write legibly while standing at an easel will write their points in light pencil, then trace over them with marker during the talk. This is a somewhat painstaking approach and may require a bit of practice in advance.

Desktop flip charts are especially useful for colorful charts and graphs, photographs, artwork and typography, and other prepared illustrations. And, of course, they are easily portable, making them especially useful for salespeople who make repeated one-on-one presentations.

Usually the graphics are enclosed in plastic sleeves. These presentation flip-chart books tend to be sturdy and designed for frequent use, unlike easel flip charts, which become dog-eared and unusable after one or two presentations.

Though useful for many kinds of business presentations, flip charts usually require the presenter to turn his or her eyes away from the audience in order turn a page or write an illustrative point. Experienced presenters learn how to write standing sideways so that contact with the audience isn't completely lost. They also keep the writing to an absolute minimum—perhaps one big word in the middle of the page—in order to maintain eye contact with their audiences.

It's also essential to write neatly and large enough for the audience to see and read easily. When the audience can't read what you've written, they'll be too distracted to hear what you have to say.

If your handwriting is awful, you should have the flip-chart pages drawn up in advance. And if your audience is larger than about thirty or forty people, another visual aid—slides or overhead transparencies, for example—will be more appropriate.

There are two little tricks used by experienced presenters that make working with flip charts easier:

1. Fold over the bottom corner of each page (do it on the side of the easel where you will be standing) into a little triangle. This becomes a kind of handle and separates the pages, making them easier to turn. An alternative to folding the page corners is to attach Post-it sheets to the bottom corner of each page on the back side.

2. When flipping the page over, pull it straight up before pulling it back over the top. The page is less likely to buckle or fold and, in addition, will make less noise.

Always keep in mind that flip chart easels aren't pieces of furniture. Nor are they particularly stable. Never lean on a flip chart—you and the chart may wind up on the floor!

Blackboards and Whiteboards

Blackboards are the classic tool for teaching presentations and they're easy and inexpensive to use. If you are presenting in a standard classroom with a blackboard, and your presentation includes a series of steps or calculations, or brainstorming, by all means use the blackboard. Make sure you have good-quality chalk and an effective eraser handy. However, blackboards are messy, and if you make the mistake of scratching the board with your nails—ugh! You've lost your audience to one of the world's worst distractions!

Whiteboards are far superior. This more up-to-date version of the blackboard is used with black and colored markers and can be easily erased. Whiteboards are easier to write on than easel-mounted flip charts. But they have the same basic disadvantages: The presenter loses eye contact with the audience when writing, and the writer must be able to write legibly. In addition, illustrations usually can't be prepared in advance, and, if they go unerased, they can be distracting. And of course, once you've filled up the space, you do have to erase it in order to go on to the next point, so you can't refer back to previous points as you can with flip-chart pages.

Easel-style whiteboards are another useful tool for presenters who like to write as they talk. Although they offer less space than a standard, wall-mounted whiteboard, the easel-style variety is easily transported and takes up little space.

Props

Props are tangible visuals—three-dimensional things you can touch or hold—and they often add life and interest—and even humor—to a presentation. Imagine a presentation on quality control to a group of employees of a company that makes tools. The presenter will make a strong impact when, one by one, he or she pulls a series of defective tools from a box.

A hands-on workshop on the topic of caring for antique linens would be hopelessly ineffective without antique linens to demonstrate with. A presentation on a building project is far more effective with a three-dimensional scale model of the building than it would be without a model. A talk on stimulating early childhood learning through play is greatly enhanced by a collection of toys and other props that illustrate the presenter's key points. And what would a presentation on first aid be without bandages, splints, ice packs, and a mannequin for demonstrating CPR?

Props don't necessarily need to be directly related to your subject matter, however. Think of the occasions when a rotten apple, a pair of dice, a dead fish, a handful of dirt, a light bulb, a map, a hundred-dollar bill, or a frying pan might make a potent impact on an audience. Consider using hats or other costumes, too, in order to make your point.

Using outrageous or unexpected props will engage your audience immediately, can add humor, and will leave a memorable impression. Of course, you need to be sure that the prop won't be offensive, that you can tie it sufficiently to your key point, and that the shock value won't cause a prolonged distraction.

Props work best with smaller audiences, say fifty or fewer. They are particularly effective for small or informal presentations where participants are seated around a conference table or in a classroom formation.

Before electing to use a prop, determine its visibility to your audience. If audience members can't see it, then the effect is lost and, chances are, so is your message. In that case, decide on another visual and save your prop idea for another time.

Other Details

Here are some things to keep in mind when planning to incorporate visual aids into your presentation:

- Visuals won't make up for a boring or poorly prepared presentation.
- Don't hand out materials that simply repeat your visuals unless you need the audience to follow along.
- Be sure the visuals you choose are appropriate to your audience and to the venue.
- Double-check all your visuals for factual errors.
- Make arrangements for transporting your visuals. Can you carry them all yourself?
- When visuals are essential to your presentation, carry them on the plane with you. Your slides will do you absolutely no good if they wind up in Cleveland and your presentation is in Chicago.

Six

Logistics

Now that we know the "who" and the "what" (and presumably the "why") of your presentation, it's time to look at the "when," the "where," and the "how." In the next few pages, we'll explore the practical logistics of planning a presentation, from choosing the right venue to deciding whether to serve food. You'll find out why Tuesday morning may be the best time to give your talk and why Friday afternoon could very well be the worst. In addition, we'll look at ways to avoid distractions, how to select a "second," what a "second" can do for you, and, perhaps one of the most important points, who pays for what.

WHEN

Time

It may be that every presentation you will ever make will be done on someone else's timetable. You are invited (instructed, commanded, directed, summoned, requested, whatever) to give a presentation at a specific time on an already determined date. It's out of your hands. Be there.

But there may be an occasion when you have some input on the scheduling of your presentation. You are in control now, and yes, the time of day does matter.

Think about a presentation you've been to that was scheduled immediately after lunch. How many people dozed? How many had to really work to keep their eyes from closing? And it's not because they were bored or disinterested. After lunch is a terrible time to present much of anything because it's the time when most people's body rhythms have dropped to a low point. Snoozing is a natural reaction to sitting still after a meal, especially if the room is warm and the lights are dimmed.

Maureen Shortt, a nutritionist who makes presentations to corporate, government, and educational groups, says that if you have to make a big presentation right after lunch, you are "dead in the water." That's because your audience will be using all of their energy on their digestion, which actually draws energy away from the brain.

People will yawn and nod off. They'll be sluggish, sleepy, and out of sorts; and depending on the amount of caffeine or alcohol they've consumed, their mood can range from antsy and fidgety to irritable, impatient, and cranky. That's just what you don't want in an audience.

An equally bad time of day is midafternoon, especially from 3 to 4 p.m. Maureen Shortt explains that during this phase of the circadian cycle of the human body, the liver is at its lowest level of performance. Many people find themselves craving caffeine, candy, or alcohol; and they are often grouchy, out of sorts, and wanting to be somewhere else. They certainly don't want to be listening to you. Unless your presentation involves lots of interaction, movement, humor, and excitement, avoid, if you can, making a postprandial or midafternoon presentation.

So what is the best time of day to make a presentation? While all of us differ to some degree in our body rhythms, most people are likely to be alert and able and willing to absorb information from 9 to 11 a.m. It's long enough after breakfast to avoid the energy-robbing digestion process, it's before hunger pangs draw minds away from the presenter, and it's still early enough in the day for people not to feel tired and worn out, and for their bottoms not to feel numb.

There may be a few individuals who don't mind, or who even enjoy an all-day presentation, but most of us feel that eight hours of presentations is too much. If you are involved in an all-day affair, chances are, unless it's a corporate training session, you'll be one of several presenters. Do your best to nab the 9-to-11 time slot. If that fails, try for the early morning session. You may miss some of the late sleepers or those who stayed in the hotel bar just a little too long the night before and are still feeling the effects, but it's more pleasant duty than the afternoon shift.

If you absolutely must make your presentation in the "dead-in-the-water" time zone, and if what you are presenting is weighty stuff that requires concentration on the part of your audience, build a few small breaks into your plan. This is a good idea for any presentation that runs longer than two hours, no matter what time of day. And a break is absolutely essential for an afternoon meeting.

The break should come at a logical point in your material. It can be as simple as an opportunity for you and your audience to stand up and stretch, go to the restroom, or get a drink of water.

While after-lunch presentations have the cards stacked against them, after-dinner presentations can go either way. If the meal is heavy and late, and your presentation is scheduled for after dessert and coffee, you're likely to lose your audience. On the other hand, if it's a social, upbeat event and your presentation is fun and entertaining, you have a good chance of keeping them with you.

Day of the Week

Here again you may not have much control over the date for your presentation. The clergy, for example, make their weekly presentations on the Sabbath; there's no getting around it. If the town council meets on Tuesday nights and you're making a presentation about your new parking meters, Tuesday night it is. And if the Rotary wants to hear your thoughts on retirement planning, you're at that meeting on Monday.

Some days of the week at some times of the year are worse than others when it comes to making a presentation, especially a presentation to a captive audience:

- Friday afternoon before a Monday-holiday weekend? Not good.
- Monday morning after New Year's? Forget it.
- Monday morning after any other holiday weekend? Probably not a great time to get people to really focus on what you're saying.

Other days that might not be the best choices to make an important presentation include:

- St. Patrick's Day? Think about it.
- Any day of the day before Christmas vacation begins? People's minds are not on work.
- The Friday before or after the Fourth of July? You're dealing with pre- or postholiday moods.
- Religious holidays (Good Friday, Yom Kippur, etc.)? You risk offending people.

Presentations made on Fridays, especially in fine weather, are at risk for losing an audience's attention. It's only human for participants to let their minds wander to upcoming weekend activities. During long corporate training sessions, it's not unusual for participants to whine and beg to be dismissed early.

If you can avoid making your presentation on Friday, do. Mondays can be difficult days, too, because many people resent the return to work after a weekend off. Or, it could be that because they've had such an awful time all weekend, they're in a rotten mood. Use Mondays with caution, and take some aspirin along.

Season

Timing a presentation for one season over another has more to do with your audience than with the time of year. For example, a fabric manufacturer would be unwise to make a sales presentation to fashion buyers at the height of the spring or fall fashion show season. His customers' minds will be on Milan and Paris, not the wonders of your woofs and warps. If your prospective client has the head of a deer mounted on his office wall, he may be too distracted to pay close attention to your presentation on the first day of hunting season. And executives at a major tourist attraction won't have much use for your advertising proposals at the beginning of their season. Where were you at the *end* of the season last year when they were examining the need to increase the number of visitors?

The business world functions year 'round. But there are a few seasonal considerations: Audiences may be thinner during the summer vacation season, particularly in July and August. If you are giving your presentation in Europe, forget August all together. The holiday season can be distracting to audiences. People will find excuses to leave early to shop, if they aren't captives. And winter storms can cause logistical problems, especially for transportation.

WHERE

Hotel, Conference Room, Restaurant . . . ?

Invited speakers, sales representatives, ad agency account executives, and corporate staffers, among others, may not have the opportunity to decide where their presentations will be delivered. Clients and prospective clients often expect presentations to be made on their turf. And when you make presentations to your superiors, subordinates, or colleagues, there's a good chance you'll do it in-house in whatever space your company uses for that purpose.

But when you have the responsibility, or at least some input, in determining the site for your presentation, you need to find a venue that will help you succeed. Before you begin a search for a presentation site, ask yourself the following questions:

- What do I want to accomplish with this presentation?
- How many people will participate?
- How long will it take?
- How much can I spend on the venue?
- What kind of technical support will I need?
- Where will participants be coming from? Will they need overnight accommodations?
- Is the presentation strictly business, or will participants expect entertaining downtime?

A sales meeting, training session, or other presentation to which participants will travel a distance can be effectively staged in an airport hotel meeting room. If it's a half-day or one-day event, participants can fly in and out the same day, saving the expenses and annoyances of overnight stays.

Suburban or center-city hotels have long been the choice for meeting and presentation sites. Serving the needs of business people has become one of the hospitality industry's primary profit generators, and there is keen competition to keep meeting room occupancy rates high. Hotels also make plenty of money on ancillary services like audiovisual equipment rentals and other logistical support.

Corporate conference rooms are appropriate sites for presentations to prospective clients. Whether you are using the prospect's space or your own space, you'll want to have a contact person there to deal with your audiovisual and other technical needs.

Consultants, sole proprietors, and owners of small businesses often contract with office suites that provide meeting space on an hourly or per-day fee basis. This is a particularly good option when it's helpful for your audience to be removed from the distractions of their home turf or when a neutral setting is more conducive to the business at hand.

Though they are appropriate for only a small segment of the business meeting pie, unique meeting locations are becoming increasingly sought after. Country inns, colleges or universities, private schools, nature centers, sports clubs, churches, and summer camps often have rooms or even entire buildings that make appropriate venues for meetings and presentations. Often located in idyllic settings, these sites provide hosts and audiences with a neutral territory away from distractions.

Joe Luccaro, owner of a country inn in Bucks County, PA, has seen growing numbers of corporate retreats, executive training sessions, and business strategy meetings in his converted-carriage-house conference center. He suggests that presenters planning a meeting in such a facility use the following venue checklist to ensure success:

- **Are the meeting rooms attractive, comfortable, and well ventilated?**
- **If participants are to stay overnight, are guest rooms attractive, comfortable, and well ventilated?**
- **Does the facility have adequate phone lines, jacks, and outlets to accommodate participants' laptop computers and modem hookups?**
- **What are the facility's audiovisual capabilities?**
- **Will there be other guests at the facility? What steps are taken to ensure privacy and quiet?**
- **What can participants do during break time? Are there exercise or entertainment options?**
- **How are meals, snacks, and coffee breaks handled? What are menu options?**

Seating Arrangements

There will be times when the setup of the room will be completely out of your hands. You'll have to make do with what you're given. But when you have input, the decisions you make about the room setup will depend on what you are presenting, the makeup of your audience, and the number in attendance.

A presentation to shareholders, who may number in the hundreds or even thousands, will take place in a large auditorium or meeting hall. This kind of presentation is usually set up theater style with fixed seats, and a podium on a stage or raised platform. And unless the presenter's style is like that of a revival meeting preacher, he isn't likely to leave the podium during the presentation. It's a static layout with few options (see Figure 6-1).

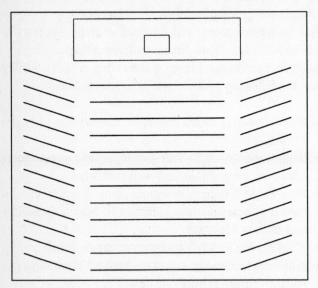

Figure 6-1. *A standard auditorium arrangement.*

Among the important variables for a theater-style presentation are the sound system and lighting. Many large theater-style venues will have a staffer familiar with these systems. You or your designee should do at last one complete run-through well in advance of the presentation to ensure the in-house systems are adequate or to check your own equipment, as well as to make certain someone has mastered the controls.

A theater-style arrangement is possible in almost any room by simply setting up the chairs in straight or chevron-shaped rows with a center aisle, side aisles, or a series of aisles separating sections of about fifteen chairs each. This is a less formal arrangement than that of a standard auditorium and is typical of presentations to civic and community organizations (see Figures 6-2 and 6-3).

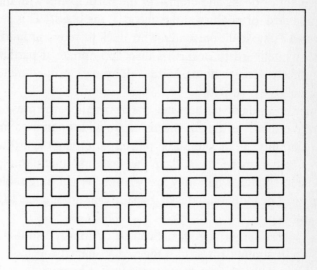

Figure 6-2. *Setting up a room like a theatre.*

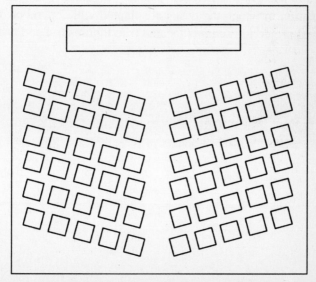

Figure 6-3. *A chevron-style arrangement.*

A classroom setup, which is appropriate for training sessions, workshops, seminars, and some informal presentations, is an arrangement of desks and chairs for the participants with the presenter at a desk or podium at the "head of the class." This setup is great for a "physical" presenter who likes to move around from easel to whiteboard to desk. It's also appropriate if participants need to take extensive notes, follow along with printed materials, or have hands-on activities.

Center and side aisles between the desks allow the presenter to "work the crowd," as long as the aisles are wide enough to maneuver comfortably. Seats should be placed far enough apart (a minimum of 2 feet, more if you have the space) so that participants' elbows don't touch when they are writing. When long tables are used instead of individual desks, be sure that no one has to straddle a table leg.

Most classroom arrangements can be customized so that desks are set up in straight rows, in staggered V-shaped rows, or in a U shape. The speaker has more opportunity for interaction with participants when rows of desks are staggered or placed in a U than if they are in straight rows. When you use staggered V-shaped rows, the direction in which the desks are slanted will depend on where the visual projection setup is located (see Figures 6-4 and 6-5).

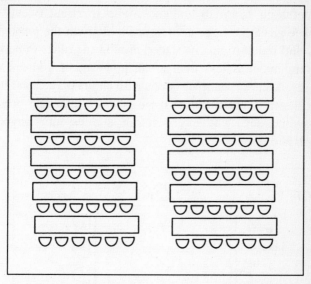

Figure 6-4. *A standard classroom arrangement.*

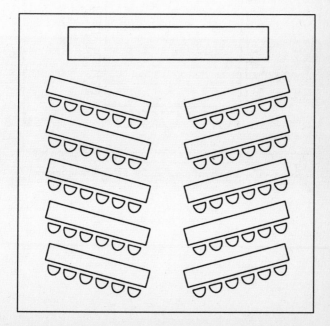

Figure 6-5. *An alternative classroom arrangement.*

103

Presentations to small audiences—up to about twenty—are often made around a large conference table with the presenter at one end and the participants seated around the other three sides. This arrangement is less than ideal, however, if you are using visual aids. A square setup of tables with chairs placed on the outside perimeter is useful when there is more than one presenter and/or for meetings where cooperation is an essential ingredient (see Figures 6-6 and 6-7).

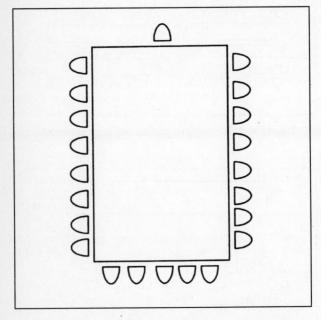

Figure 6-6. *A standard conference table arrangement.*

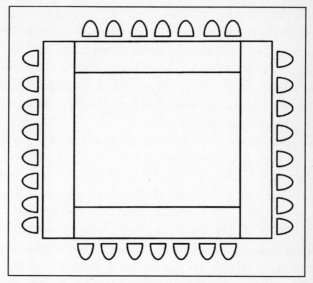

Figure 6-7. *A square setup of conference tables.*

The T-shaped setup is essentially a head table with an intersecting perpendicular table set with chairs on both sides. This arrangement is typical of some formal presentations such as awards banquets and retirement dinners (see Figure 6-8).

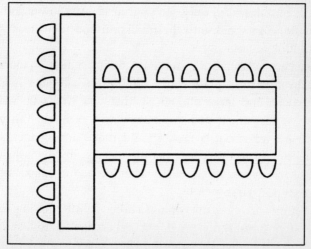

Figure 6-8. *A T-shaped setup of conference tables.*

PODIUMS AND MICROPHONES

Podiums and lecterns as basically the same thing. A lectern is a reading desk with a slanted top used in churches to hold the books from which Scriptural passages are read during a church service. Additionally, the term is used for any stand that supports notes. A podium is essentially the same, but is also defined as an elevated platform for a public speaker.

Many presentation formats include the use of a podium or lectern, so you should be familiar with their use. (There's more on presentation formats in Chapter 3.) Podiums and lecterns are often free-standing pieces of furniture with shelves on the side facing the speaker and a solid panel facing the audience. Often they are equipped with a light and fitted with a microphone. The slanted desktop should have a lip that serves to prevent the speaker's notes from sliding off. And often a pitcher of water and a glass are placed on one of the shelves. Another lectern style consists of a stand with nothing more than the lip to hold notes.

One of the main concerns for a speaker when working with a podium is its height. For the very short or the very tall, the standard podium height may be awkward. For comfort and appearance, a podium should come to about the middle of your chest. Any higher and you'll have to strain to see your notes and the audience, and they will only see your head. Any lower and you'll have to stoop to speak into the mike and bob your head up and down to look at your notes.

Presenters who are shorter than about 5 feet 4 inches tall should arrange for a platform to stand on. Make sure it is completely stable and large enough so that you won't be worrying about what happens if you step backward too much. Tall presenters, those over about 6 feet, should make arrangements for a taller podium or to raise the existing one. Again, any adjustments should be sturdy and reliable. However, no podium should ever be used to support your weight.

Sometimes using a microphone takes a little getting used to. Unless we do it regularly, we might feel compelled to lean into the microphone or to speak louder than necessary.

New audio equipment is extremely sensitive, so the speaker needs only to speak in a normal voice for adequate amplification. More sophisticated systems will use remote, battery-operated mikes. The battery pack can be concealed in your pocket or attached to your belt or waistband. A wire with the mike usually goes under your clothing and is attached with a small clip to a shirt or jacket. These are the easiest mikes to use and give the speaker the freedom to move around.

There are also hand-held, remote microphones. These are the kind Oprah, Sally, Leeza, and other TV talk-show hosts use when they walk among the audience members to get their opinions. Working with this kind of mike is a little more difficult. The speaker must talk directly into the mike in order for the voice to be amplified. Thus, the talk-show host asks a question into the mike, and then puts the mike in front of the other person's mouth.

If you are using a hand-held microphone, remember that no one will hear you unless you speak directly into it. Remote mikes allow you the same kind of freedom to move around as the battery-pack clip-on mikes, but they restrict you to the use of one hand (while the other holds the mike), though they can be mounted on a pole or desk.

Less advanced hand-held mikes have long cords that are easy to trip over. If your presentation venue uses this kind of mike, you may want to limit your movements, or even remain at the podium or stand where the mike can be securely mounted.

Many podiums are fitted with a microphone on a flexible metal arm. The difficulty with them is that sometimes the arm isn't as secure as it should be and the microphone will begin to droop. Sometimes microphones have their own desktop stand. These are more commonly used in a panel discussion format or at a meeting with a U- or T-shaped setup.

Check the microphone well before your appearance, and have any adjustments that you need made well in advance. The microphone head should be about a foot to 18 inches from your mouth. And it's always a good idea to do a sound check early enough in the day to have repairs or adjustments made before you are scheduled to speak.

ASSIGN A SECOND

When a man was challenged to a duel, he always brought along his second, who served as his assistant. The second, sometimes a friend, but often a trusted and valued servant, carried the sword or pistol and helped the dueler prepare. He was also handy for bandaging a wound or hauling the remains away.

Your second won't have to deal with mortal wounds, but his or her duties can be critically important. Your second may be your secretary or assistant, a colleague, your client, a junior staffer, a partner, a friend, or even a spouse, depending on your situation and the circumstances surrounding your presentation.

What does the second do? His or her tasks are varied and essential. A second's duties may include:

- Assisting with research
- Listening to and timing your talk
- Providing feedback on content, visuals, and your appearance and voice in advance of the presentation
- Accompanying you to the presentation (perhaps driving and parking the car, helping with luggage and equipment, etc.)
- Helping you set up
- Serving as liaison with venue staffers
- Greeting participants
- Assisting with visuals during the presentation (advancing slides, running the computer for computer-generated graphics, turning the VCR on and off)
- Dimming the lights
- Serving as gatekeeper (see below)

Unless you are highly placed in your organization or have a devoted assistant, or your only job is to make presentations, it is unlikely that your second will perform all these tasks. You may have to call on many different people to help you. Your wife, husband, or child might time and critique your talk; a client's junior staffer might be assigned to run your slides, and a friend in the audience, who has been briefed in advance, could handle the lights for you.

When your second serves as a gatekeeper, he or she is like the hall monitor at school—someone who is all eyes and ears and ready to troubleshoot, who remains unobtrusive, but is always there when needed. His or her major roles include dealing with distractions (which you'll read about later in this chapter) and interacting with others (hotel or meeting venue staff, technicians, transportation and other vendors, and sometimes your office).

DISTRACTIONS

Work is hard. Distractions are plentiful. And time is short.

—ADAM HOCHSCHILD

Human beings are easily distracted. Most of us are used to concentrating for relatively long periods of time, but few of us can resist an interesting or startling distraction. Our attention might stray to the news on TV while we should be holding up our end of a conversation with a spouse. We might be distracted by a conversation between two coworkers in the hall just outside the office, instead of paying heed to the client on the phone. Or the sight of a very attractive person across the room in a restaurant might prevent us from hearing what our lunch companion has just said.

Distractions happen!

Losing an audience to nearby distractions is one of the most unnerving of experiences to the presenter. And sometimes it just can't be prevented:

- A waiter drops an entire tray of glasses just as you make a key point.
- A latecomer makes an entrance and proceeds to greet his twenty best friends.
- A participant falls asleep and begins to snore loudly.
- No one can find the dimmer switch for the lights, causing a delay in presenting your slides.
- The sound system or the VCR doesn't work.
- Food-service personnel decide to refill the coffee urns just as you are making your call to action.
- Hotel staffers begin to set up for a wedding in the next room, and you've only just begun the most detailed part of your talk.

When distractions happen, your job as a presenter is to take ownership of the situation, diffuse the distractions, and continue with your presentation. (Strategies for dealing with logistical distractions and those caused by rude, disruptive, hostile, or negative participants are addressed in Chapter 9.)

The best defense against logistical distractions is an offensive position—don't allow them to happen in the first place. Of course, there are distractions over which you have no control at all. But if you are involved in the planning of your presentation, or if you have a cooperative relationship with your host or client, you can plan against distractions by doing the following:

- Assign a gatekeeper.
- Select a venue that offers soundproof meeting rooms.
- Arrive early enough to try out all the technical equipment.
- Have spare parts for equipment on hand.

- Discuss your technical and support requirements in detail with whomever is responsible for them.
- Let the venue management know that any distracting noise from adjacent rooms or hallways is not acceptable to you.

WHO PAYS?

Though there will always be exceptions, there is a general rule in determining who picks up the tab for presentations. Essentially, the tab is paid by whoever initiates the presentation.

For example, an advertising agency or a training organization will approach a potential client and offer to make a presentation. They are looking to sell their services, so they pay the expenses. An exception, and there are always exceptions, is when the client routinely trains on-site and will be making the presentation there.

A speaker fee is frequently called an honorarium, which is defined as "a payment given to a professional for services in situations where fees are not regularly or legally required." Honoraria are frequently paid to academic and scholarly types who speak outside their usual venues. Some speakers derive their entire incomes from honoraria (and yes, the right word is *honoraria* for more than one *honorarium*).

When an insurance company asks a motivational speaker to address its agents at a national sales convention, all the speaker's expenses, including travel, hotel, meals, and audiovisual rentals, will be paid for by the host company. The speaker, in most cases, will provide his or her own slides and handouts.

An independent contractor making a presentation to a corporate client may be reimbursed for expenses. It depends on the company's policy and the arrangement that has been agreed on in advance.

There are, of course, innumerable occasions when the lines are a little fuzzy. For example, the presentation to the public of a proposal by an architectural firm for a school building plan might include the cost of overheads, explanatory packets for school board members, handouts for the general public, easel and paper, and overtime pay for the custodians. In this case, the presenting firm will surely pay for the visuals and the packets for board members. The school board might make the copies for the public, will probably provide the easel with paper, and will pick up the overtime pay for the custodians. The important thing is to spell out, well in advance, who pays for what.

If you are invited to be a guest speaker, confirm all the arrangements in a letter that should look something like this:

Dear Ms. McCabe:

I am looking forward to giving my talk on the opportunities for the hospitality industry in the Pacific Rim on October 22 at 7 p.m. at your dinner meeting.

My understanding is that I will make my own travel arrangements and invoice you for the expenses, along with any out-of-pocket expenses. You will have a driver meet me at the airport in Seattle, and you will arrange for a car to return me to the airport the following day. In addition, you will make the hotel reservation, which will be billed to you by the hotel.

It is also my understanding that the honorarium, in the amount of $1000, will be mailed to me within fifteen days of my talk.

Please let me know if you have any additional requests for specific areas of content for the talk.

Sincerely,

Marcia L. Cooper

There. It's clearly spelled out leaving no room for misunderstanding.

For a small, get-to-know-each-other meeting, where you will be presenting your product, service, or expertise in an informal setting over lunch or dinner, be prepared to pick up the tab unless you've established in advance that someone else will. In this instance, you are essentially playing host, so you should arrive ahead of your guests and instruct the waiter or maitre d' that the check will go to you.

WHEN AND WHAT DO WE EAT?

Here's the dilemma: If coffee or food is served *before* a presentation, participants might become sleepy or agitated. If refreshments are offered *during* a talk, the noise of serving and eating will distract the audience. If a meal is served *after* a presentation, the anticipation might keep the audience from listening. And if nothing at all is served, participants may feel cheated.

Unfortunately, food is often more important to us than we would like to admit. Some folks start to think fondly of lunch as they're drinking the last of their breakfast OJ. There are those who live for coffee breaks. For others, thoughts of food bring on anxious feelings: What if I don't like what's being served? Will there be a salt-free selection? I hope they don't offer chocolate desserts!

Food—whether or not it is served at your presentation—puts you in a no-win situation. It is, however, possible to minimize the disadvantages and distractions caused by serving refreshments and still meet the food-related expectations and needs of your audience.

If coffee service is included in your presentation plan, try to schedule it before or after you speak. Nutritionist Maureen Shortt recommends offering herbal teas and decaf coffee, as well as tea, juices, fruit, and yogurt, along with the usual Danish and coffee because, she explains, healthy snacks tend to make people better listeners. Serving refreshments before your presentation has the added benefit of giving people something to do while they are settling in. This is especially helpful when participants are strangers to each other.

When serving refreshments before your presentation, arrange for service carts to be removed from the room before you begin. You don't want to compete with the noise and movement of food-service staffers. And this way members of your audience won't get up during your talk to help themselves to another cup of coffee.

An even better arrangement is to have the food service in an adjacent room that can be closed off before you start your talk. Be sure to inform the venue staff that they may not clear that room until you have finished speaking, unless it is fully soundproof.

There are occasions when food will be served during your presentation. An informal, get-to-know-each-other meeting where you are more or less presenting yourself rather than a program, project, or proposal is often more comfortable when done during a dinner or lunch. All-day presentations, in-house training sessions, small group meetings, and informal presentations might include an on-site meal. These situations are roll-your-sleeves-up occasions at which sandwich trays or box lunches are appropriate, and appreciated by the participants.

If you will be making a presentation during such a meeting, put off eating until after you have done your part. If that's not possible, eat sparingly, and avoid high-fat foods that take a lot of energy to digest. Have fruit and bread, but stay away from meats and mayo. You want to be alert when it's your turn to speak. In a restaurant, order something that is easy to eat; don't order a meal that requires a lot of cutting with a knife or is potentially messy. And remember what your mother taught you about chewing your food well. Finally, avoid drinking alcoholic beverages, as they can compromise your mental agility.

I had my first meeting with my first prospective client, a bank, a month after I started a public relations consulting business. The bank's representatives included the public relations director and the assistant director, who was a former colleague of mine. I was excited and jittery about making a good impression on my friend's boss. Often when I'm nervous, I eat; so naturally, when the waitress served a basket of bread, I helped myself. A small crumb went down the wrong way and within seconds I was choking enough to frighten my lunch companions and to be offered the Heimlich maneuver by half a dozen diners seated nearby. After a few minutes of coughing and sputtering, I regained control of my throat and, though excruciatingly embarrassed, did my best to restore some kind of businesslike demeanor. The bank eventually became a wonderful client, but I can still feel the intensity of my embarrassment nearly two decades later. To this day, I don't eat bread if I'm even a little nervous.

GET THERE ON TIME

Eighty percent of success is showing up.
—WOODY ALLEN

The plane (train, bus, limo) was late.
My flight was canceled.
There was an accident on the turnpike.

I had an accident.
I got lost.
The hotel forgot my wakeup call.
My car wouldn't start.

When it comes to being late to give a presentation, or—God forbid, missing it altogether—there are only two acceptable excuses: a death in the family and extreme sickness or injury. The well-prepared, professional presenter will always add "just-in-case" time to the schedule. If your talk is scheduled for early morning, plan to stay the night before. If the venue is in a part of town you don't know, do a test drive a week early to see how much time it takes to get there. If you have a lot of things to set up, give yourself an extra hour or two in case you need to track down a porter or an electrician.

A few years ago during a media tour, I was booked to appear on an early morning TV news show in St. Louis. I was traveling with a young and somewhat inexperienced PR woman who had arranged the bookings. The night before we had stayed in a downtown hotel that, according to the travel agent, was only a few blocks from the television studio. And we were up and out of the hotel with what should have been plenty of time before my appointment.

But, despite the fact that the hotel was only a mile from our destination, and we had been given directions by someone at the TV station, we became hopelessly lost. There was no direct route from the hotel, and we found ourselves in a confusion of limited-access highway and one-way streets. Eventually, we found the building and parked the car, only to find the entrance locked (it was, after all, 5:45 a.m.). By the time we walked three-quarters of the way around the block in a freezing and dark downtown, I had missed the live interview.

How can you prevent such a disaster? You can think ahead, ask the right questions, and add "just-in-case" time to your schedule.

Here are some steps to take in order to avoid an inexcusable calamity:

- Ask your host to send or fax you detailed directions, including a map.
- Ask about parking specifics.
- If your arrival time is outside normal business hours, determine how you will enter the site.
- Ask who will be there to greet you and get that person's phone number.
- Find out if there is an after-hours phone number.
- Have names and phone numbers of several other people who might be able to assist you (for example, your host, his or her secretary or assistant, a manager of the venue, or your hotel concierge).
- Carry a cellular phone with fresh batteries.
- If possible, make a dry run the day before.
- If you are told that it takes ten minutes to get from the hotel to the destination, allow a half hour.
- Plan alternative transportation. If you are driving, have the phone numbers handy for a limo service and taxi. Memorize the phone number for your travel agent or the person who handles your travel arrangements so that you can have alternative reservations made quickly. If there is a flight delay, be aware of other flights.
- If you sense that you are lost or the directions are incomplete or incorrect, call someone at your destination immediately. There may be occasions when you need to be "walked through" directions in order to find where you are going.
- Keep in touch with your own office or with someone at the phone number at which you are usually reached. Your host will feel far more secure if he or she knows that someone knows where you are.

Robert Grumet, an archaeologist, was scheduled to address a session of the Society of American Archaeology at their annual meeting in New Orleans. His presentation was to be on a Friday, and he arrived at his hotel on Wednesday, giving him more than adequate "just-in-case" time. On Thursday, he found himself in a New Orleans hospital emergency room with two herniated disks requiring lots of painkillers and eventual surgery. This was an acceptable excuse. Despite his considerable pain, Robert did, however, arrange for someone to take over and give his presentation. Robert is a first-rate, experienced presenter. The fact that he did not leave his prospective audience without a presenter is a significant sign of his professionalism.

OTHER DETAILS

Here are a few more tips that will help you avoid a crisis:

- Check the lighting. Is there enough light? Can it be adjusted? Do you know where the light switches are? Is the podium lighted so you can see your notes?
- Be sure that someone knows how to turn off the Muzak.
- If you find that attendance is significantly smaller than you had originally expected, rearrange the seating so that you aren't faced with an acre of empty chairs.
- Have the phone number of the person to call if the room is too cold or too hot.
- If you are presenting slides, be sure the room can be sufficiently darkened.
- Are there enough restrooms?
- Is there a coat room? Are there enough hangers?

Accept the fact that no presentation venue is perfect and something may go wrong. The only solution is to keep your sense of humor and captivate your audience!

THE PRESENTER'S EMERGENCY KIT

When my family takes a vacation, especially one that takes us a long distance from home, my husband and I scurry around the house searching for important small items and trying to make mental lists of everything we could possibly need while we're gone. Do we have the Benedryl for an allergy attack? Where's the aspirin? Address book? Sunscreen? Band-Aids and antiseptic cream? We think about every little thing that could go wrong and try to pack an antidote.

It's a good idea for presenters to think like parents. "What do I need to have on hand just in case something goes wrong, breaks, gets lost, or otherwise fails me?" should be one of the questions you ask yourself in advance of your presentation.

The following list will help you develop your own Presenter's Emergency Kit. First, think about the personal you. What back-ups and remedies might you need to have within easy reach?

- Toothbrush and toothpaste, dental floss
- A small hand mirror
- Small makeup kit with just the basics, such as lipstick, blush, mascara, and perhaps coverup for a blemish
- A comb
- A spare shirt and tie or blouse and scarf
- An extra pair of panty hose
- A nail file
- Tissues

- Aspirin
- Antidiarrheal medicine (you never know!)
- Antacids
- A small sewing kit
- Manicure scissors

What else might help you solve a logistics problem?

- A spare bulb for your projector
- An extension cord
- A voltage adapter (three-prong to two-prong)
- A flashlight
- Batteries
- Scissors
- A small set of screwdrivers
- Extra pens, pencils, paper

And be sure to pack:

- Business cards
- Address book

Seven

Write for Speaking

The words of language resemble the strings of a musical instrument, which yield only uninteresting tones when struck by an ordinary hand, but from which a skillful performer draws forth the soul of harmony, awakening and captivating the passions of the mind.

—W. B. CLULOW

Presentations are almost always written, in some form or another, before they are spoken. Sure, there are some highly experienced presenters who can successfully deliver a forty-five-minute presentation completely off the cuff. But even these old pros surely wrote something down—an outline, a few lines on note cards, or a few thoughts on a cocktail napkin—when they made the presentation the first time.

Unfortunately, the fear of writing is almost as prevalent as the fear of speaking in public, and some poor souls are plagued by both phobias. Writing doesn't just happen. Most good writers spend a long time developing their craft and perfecting their skills. But, with a little review of good writing principles, almost anyone can write well enough to prepare a successful presentation. In Chapter 3, we talked about preparing an outline or a mind map to organize a presentation. Here we'll look at other aspects of writing for speaking.

Although a presentation is essentially the act of rendering the written word in oral form, the presence of the written word isn't excluded from the actual presentation. In fact, most presentations, particularly in the business arena, will include the distribution of handouts, mainly in the form of written materials. In this chapter, we'll also see how the written word is incorporated into your presentation, and what purpose it serves. And we'll look at ways to make our language as bias free as possible and thereby avoid causing offense or hurt feelings.

ACTION, PLEASE!

Can you define the difference between the active and the passive voice in written or spoken language? Maybe not, but I know you'll be able to identify it when you see it.

Here are two ways of saying the same thing: (1) The results of our market research have been tabulated and analyzed and are to be presented to the board at its next meeting. (2) We have tabulated and analyzed the results of our market research, and we will present them to the board at its next meeting.

The first sentence is written in the passive voice. The subject is acted on. The second example is written in the active voice. The subject acts: We did this. We will do that. The active voice is strong, forceful, engaging, take-charge, responsible. The passive voice is, well, passive—weak, unwilling to take responsibility, evasive.

Presenters should always strive to use the active voice when they write or otherwise prepare their presentations. But for people who are used to protecting their posteriors with obscure, hedging, careful words, the passive voice is a way of life: Things are done and policies are made and orders have been received and steps are being taken and things are being looked into. When you make a policy or do things or take steps or look into things, you are doing the action, taking the risk, and handling the task. That is your active voice. Use it!

To guard against the passive voice slipping back into your presentation, examine your words by asking yourself, "Who is doing what here?" If the subject of your point is having something done to it, that's passive. Turn the thought around and put the action back into your words. The following expressions will lead you into passivity, so don't use them:

- It has been reported that . . .
- It goes without saying that . . .
- It is widely considered to be . . .
- It's worth noting that . . .
- It is suggested that . . .

There are, however, times when a passive voice is appropriate. This usually happens when the action is more important than the person or thing that is doing the action. For example, awards are presented, companies are started, people are laid off, land is sold, and consensus has been reached.

BIAS-FREE LANGUAGE

The issue of bias in language is a land mine waiting to be stepped on. It started, more or less, in the 1960s, and by the 90s the need to be politically correct became, for some, an obsession. There are those who cringe inside, but wouldn't dream of objecting, when they hear an insensitive type talk about manning the exhibit at a trade show or about how many man-hours it takes to accomplish a task. Other, more outspoken people might voice an objection, but most people will hear the offensive language, keep their council, and remember the speaker with disfavor. Whatever your level of concern with this issue, as a presenter you must recognize that there is the potential to offend people, and you should work at minimizing that possibility.

Take, for example, this quote from Braude's *Source Book for Speakers & Writers*: "Women have a better business sense than men. . . . When her business is to catch a man, she doesn't sit around criticizing the government. She spends half her time in beauty parlors and the other half out where eligible men can be found." No one would dream of using that quote today. It is far too offensive. Yet in 1968, when the book was published, it was probably considered hilarious.

And how about this one: "Don't dare underestimate the customer for one second. He has a brain and he can use it. The old saying, 'Simple men believe everything they hear; and smart men want proof,' is not an accurate rule of thumb. All customers are thinkers; they know more than you believe they do." This is sage advice. However, the writer makes the assumption that customers are all men. Perhaps it's an unintentional, automatic thing, or maybe it was written that way for expediency. This quote, from James W. Pickens' classic book, *The Art of Closing Any Deal*, with over a million copies sold, has helped countless people in their sales efforts. And that edition was published in 1989, when you would have thought that the editors would know better; but, in fact, the book is full of biased language.

How can we fix the situation? It's not that difficult. Let's rewrite Picken's advice about customers: "Don't dare underestimate your customers for one second. They have brains and know how to use them. Remember the old saying, 'Simple people believe everything they hear; and smart people want proof.'" See how easy it is to change the language so that it is more inclusive and less likely to offend.

Keep in mind that gender bias is not the only area you can get in trouble with in language usage. Marilyn Schwartz, along with the other members of the Task Force on Bias-Free Language of the Association of American University Presses, has written a small, but important book, *Guidelines for Bias-Free Writing*, that may be as important as *The Elements of Style* or *The Elements of Business Writing* for the writer and presenter. And although the issue of gender accounts for forty-two pages of a one-hundred-page book, there are several other areas to consider when you are preparing your presentation. Among the most important are race, ethnicity, religion, medical conditions and disabilities, sexual orientation, and age.

Here are some things to keep in mind:

- The words *older person* or *older people* are preferable to *elderly, senior citizens*, or *old people*.
- Be aware of courtesy titles (Mr., Miss, Mrs., Ms.) when addressing or referring to someone. The "Mr." part is easy; but to find out which title a woman prefers, you have to ask. If you don't have the opportunity to ask, you may need to use the woman's full name when you speak of her.
- Don't use what the *Guidelines* authors call "default assumptions." This happens when we make the assumption that a class or group of people is all male or all female. For example, a school principal may use the pronoun *she* when talking about parents or may use *mother* and *parent* interchangeably, or a speaker may refer to a physician by the pronoun *he*.
- Avoid sexist words such as the following: *stewardess, workman* or *working man, mailman, actress, policeman, chairman, housewife*, and *maiden name*. Use these instead: *flight attendant, worker, wage earner*, or *employee, mail carrier, actor, police officer, chair* or *chairperson, homemaker*, and *birth name* or *former name*.
- Use *place of worship* instead of the broader and Christian-oriented word *church*, unless you are actually talking about a church.
- Avoid default assumptions about race. The *Guidelines* use this example of bad form: *two men and a black woman*. It would be better to write (or say) either *two white men and a black woman* or *two men and a woman*.
- Avoid race, religious, or ethnic imagery in language when its use implies a negative synonym or corollary. Some commonly used terms that should be banished

from presentation vocabulary include *black-hearted* (and similar expressions), *pure white* or *lily white*, *flesh colored*, *white trash*, and *good Christian values*.

- Expressions like *welshing on a deal*, *getting gypped*, *getting the Irish up*, *Dutch treat*, *Mexican standoff*, and other derogatory ethnic or cultural references should also be banned.

- Be sensitive to words used in connection with disabilities, medical conditions, and diseases. For example, avoid making victims of people by saying things such as *suffering with* (a disease), *a victim of* (a medical condition), or *confined to a wheelchair*.

- And don't use words like *deformed*, *crippled*, *defective*, or *invalid*. The writers of the bias-free guidelines encourage writers (and I urge speakers) to emphasize positive things by using words such as *survivor* or *wheelchair user*.

WORD ALERT!

You don't need decorated words to make your meanin' clear. Say it plain and save some breath for breathin'.

—TEXAS BIX BINDER

Most of us are guilty, at least once in a while, of using five words when one good one will do. And few of us can say that we never or rarely use jargon. Being concise, direct, and to the point are virtues that few people can consistently claim. But presenters need to work toward cleaning up their language to avoid redundancies (see the next section), overused, cheesy expressions and clichés, malapropisms, wordiness, and an overdependence on jargon and buzz words. It's a good idea to get in the habit of streamlining your vocabulary in order to eliminate expressions, words, and unnecessary jargon that fill up space and time without adding meaning or information.

Here are a few expressions that you won't miss once you get rid of them:

- It was deemed necessary (this is also a passive voice phrase)
- In point of fact
- The fact of the matter is
- In actuality
- It's been deemed inadvisable (does anyone really "deem" anything more?)
- It is my considered opinion—which is worse than
- To the best of my recollection—but not as bad as
- For all intents and purposes

Jargon and slang are okay to use only if you know for sure that the entire audience is familiar with the words you are using. For example, if you are addressing a group of nursery managers, it's all right to talk about their IPM (Integrated Pest Management) plans or about the price of arbs (arborvitae). And if everyone in the audience is a psychologist or psychiatrist, you can go right ahead and use genogram (family history tree), MDD (Major Depressive Disorder), or DID (Dissociative Disorder) without hesitation, because you know they'll know what you're talking about. But, for more heterogeneous audiences, you may need to explain what your verbal shorthand means, at least once or twice, before using it freely in your presentation.

IT'S DÉJÀ VU ALL OVER AGAIN

I'm pretty tolerant of most gaffes made by presenters, but there's one sin that I find almost unforgivable—the use of redundancies. Something is redundant when (according to the American

Heritage Dictionary) it (1) exceeds what is necessary or natural, is superfluous; or (2) is needlessly repetitive or verbose. Unfortunately, too many people think that more of a good thing is better. When it comes to language, less is almost always more.

Gary Blake and Robert W. Bly, authors of *The Elements of Business Writing*, compiled an extensive list of the most common redundancies. Many redundancies also fall under the category of clichés, another speakers' taboo. Here are some of Blake and Bly's top offenders, with a few I love to hate, with words or phrases to use in their place:

very unique	unique
absolute truth	the truth
tiny, little	tiny (or little or very small)
joined together	joined (or together)
actual experience	experience
an honor and a privilege	an honor (or a privilege)
current status	status
combine into one	combine
any and all	all
basic essentials	basics (or essentials)
final outcome	outcome
first priority	priority
one and the same	the same
point in time	time
past history	history
refer back to	refer to
new breakthrough	breakthrough
final outcome	outcome

Look out for words that make you sound as if you're trying to be smart but often make you seem pretentious,
or worse, dumb. H. A. Lechevalier, a professor emeritus at
the Waksman Institute at Rutgers University, developed a
guide to correct language usage. Dr. Lechevalier's reference was created for the scientific community, which is
notorious for linguistic horrors, but the following list of
words taken from his guide, along with a few of my personal favorites, will offer language protection to presenters in any field:

ABOLISHMENT—This is not a real word. Use *abolition*
instead.

ADMINISTRATE—This is another nonword. The better
word is *administer*.

AGGRAVATE—*Aggravate* actually means "to make
worse." So, "your headache is aggravated by irritating [not aggravating] interruptions."

ANTICIPATE—You probably mean *expect*. Use *anticipate* when you want to say you will "act before." For
example, "We anticipated the severe winter and
increased our fuel contracts."

ANXIOUS—The misuse of this word is at the top of my
father's pet peeve list! Use *anxious* only when you
mean "filled with anxiety or worry." You probably
mean to use *eager* when you want to say that you
are "enthusiastic about doing something" or "going
somewhere."

COMPOSED and COMPRISE—These are a little tricky.
Use *composed* with the word *of* and use *comprised*
alone. For example, "The unit was composed of
seven design teams." and "The unit comprised
seven design teams."

CONTINUOUS and CONTINUAL—These two words are
often used interchangeably (and wrongly). *Continuous*

means "something happens without stopping." *Continual* means "it happens frequently." There's a big difference.

ELUCIDATE—This is a $5 word when $1 words such as *analyze, establish,* or *work out* will do. The literal translation is "to cast light on," and it's a good word, but often used pretentiously.

FUNCTIONALITY—Spare me from this jargon. What about the plain old word *functional*!

HOPEFULLY—This is an adverb and should only be used as such. For example, "We looked hopefully toward a positive end-of-year report." "Hopefully we'll have a positive end-of-year report" is wrong.

LESS and FEWER—Use *fewer* when you are talking about things that can be counted; *less* has to do with mass or space. For example, "We will have less waste if we have fewer errors in accounting."

IRREGARDLESS—This is among the worst offenders. The right word is *regardless*.

LOCALIZE and LOCATE—*Localize* means something is "confined to one specific location." For example, "The infestation has been localized to one warehouse." *Locate* means "to find the location of something." For example, "The operations manager has located the entry point for the infestation."

MOMENTARILY—*Momentarily* means "lasting only a brief time." So if you say "I'll address that momentarily" it doesn't mean that you'll get to that issue in a minute. It means that you'll only give it a moment of your time.

ORIENTATE—There is no such word. Try *orient* and *oriented* instead.

PREVENTATIVE—Use *preventive* when you need an adjective, and the longer word when a noun is called for. For example, "We need to take preventive measures in order to protect our computer system." But "He took an indigestion preventative."

PRIORITIZE—The word *prioritize* is a favorite of bureaucrats! Use *set priorities* or *order* instead.

STRATEGIZE—*Strategize* is almost as bad as *prioritize*. Try *plan a strategy*.

UNIQUE—This overused word has lost its uniqueness. Use *unique* only when you mean "one of a kind." Never use *sort of unique*. It's like being sort of pregnant. *Very unique* is also a no-no.

WHY GIVE HANDOUTS?

The primary reasons to give handouts to your audience is to clarify your message, to make it easier to understand, and to reinforce your key points. If your presentation is designed to inform your audience, then your handouts will add to your information, providing greater depth or support for it. If your hope is to persuade your audience with your presentation, handout materials should reinforce that persuasive message.

Here are some examples of the appropriate use of handout materials:

- The school board will hand out a complete budget at a public hearing on next year's proposed budget.
- A juvenile social worker, when addressing a group of parents, will pass out a list of warning signs to look for when a child is using drugs.
- An ad agency executive will give her clients their own photocopies of the story boards of a new TV campaign she is presenting.
- A pharmaceutical executive will include specific clinical-trial results in a packet of information on a new over-the-counter drug.

- A union official will give his audience a sheet comparing wages in his industry with those paid in similar fields.
- A salesperson will give her prospect a written proposal asking for an order following her presentation.

WHAT TO HAND OUT

Written handouts include, but are not limited to the following:

- Lists
- Charts and graphs
- Copies of the visuals to be presented
- A synopsis of the presentation
- An outline of the presentation
- Suggested reading
- A proposal
- Supporting documents
- An agenda
- A budget
- Workbooks

There are also handouts that may include the written word, but are something else entirely:

- Videotapes
- Product samples
- Pens, pencils, calculators, calendars, notebooks, baseball caps, and other premiums (that is, promotional materials)

These handouts are often used to emphasize a sales message and leave the audience with something tangible to remind them of the presenter's proposal, product, idea, or service.

PRESENT THE WRITTEN WORD

You may hand out a copy of everything you plan to say or a typed version of all your visuals. But this can be counterproductive. The audience may become so caught up in reading your materials that they won't pay attention to you. And some may become distracted trying to find where in the packet of materials you are at the moment, creating distractions for everyone around them as they rustle through a pile of papers. Instead, an outline, a brief, a synopsis, or an abbreviated list might better serve your purpose and your audience.

Your handout materials should be of the same high quality as your visuals. Have pages laser printed, offset printed, or, at least, copied on a high-resolution copy machine. Be sure that the visuals contained in your printed material are clear and not smudged or blurred. Better to leave out photos if they don't reproduce well.

If you want your audience to take notes, and research shows that note-taking audience members seem to become more involved in presentations and retain more information than non-note-takers, you should construct your handout materials with plenty of space for notes. A well-planned outline or synopsis with plenty of white space is one way to do it. Or you can give each audience member a ring binder or spiral-bound notebook with additional blank pages. This will give people adequate space for writing their own notes.

Avoid handing participants a bunch of loose papers, because they may wind up scattered around the floor with participants on their hands and knees trying to retrieve them. If your presentation includes handing out pages at different points in your talk, give people folders or have holes punched in the handouts so they can be added to the ring binders. However, people can make distracting noises opening and closing ring binders. Ask them to hold off on that task until break time.

HANDOUTS AS PROSPECTING TOOLS

You may remember the stockbroker, described in Chapter 4, who handed out cards to audience members as they entered the room. He asked the participants to write a question for him on the cards, but then used his own set of cards during his presentation.

The "card trick" is a clever mechanism for making the audience feel involved in the presentation; it's also a great way to build a mailing list. Postcards can provide a painless way to gather the names of interested participants, in order to build a mailing or prospect list, especially when you have no other source. It's a nice touch to reward those who do take the time to fill out cards. The reward can be some kind of gift or remembrance—perhaps a pen, a notebook, a baseball cap, or some other appropriate premium (for example, additional information that may be of interest to them). This is an especially good idea if you want or need to build a relationship with these people.

The postcard could have preprinted on it a request form for additional support materials to be mailed to the participant; or something as simple as "Do you want to keep in touch?"—which will help you identify people predisposed to developing a relationship with you.

BEFORE OR AFTER . . . WHEN TO GIVE THEM THE PRINTED STUFF

When should you hand out printed materials? Should you hand out material before your talk, and then hope the audience won't be distracted because they are reading the handouts instead of listening to the speaker? Or should you hand out material after the presentation, and then hope the material will remain relevant and the audience will actually look at it? Your decision should depend on the format of your meeting, what it is that you are handing out, and what your audience expects to receive from you.

For small meetings, where the audience members will sit at classroom-style tables or around a conference table, you should consider placing a packet of your handout materials at each seat before the participants arrive. Be prepared, human nature being what it is, for most people to open their packets immediately and peruse the contents. That's fine when people arrive early and have plenty of time to look through the materials before they settle in to hear your presentations. Late arrivals, however, will tend to be distracted or cause others to become distracted because they too will want to look through the materials, even though you may have already begun your presentation.

The only surefire way to deal with the possibility of this kind of distraction is to wait until everyone has arrived before you begin. That, however, isn't always feasible. You could have your second ask a tardy participant to refrain from opening his packet until the break or until you ask the participants to turn to the first page. But chances are he'll open the packet anyway as soon as he or she sits down.

An additional reason for handing out printed materials before your presentation is so that people can follow along. This is particularly useful when your presentation includes complicated, hard-to-understand, or very precise information that your audience members will need to retain. Because there are so many learning styles, you will reach more people if you present your material both orally and visually.

If it's vital that the audience pays strict attention at a given point in your presentation, it's perfectly acceptable for you to instruct them to put the handouts aside and concentrate on what you have to say or focus on the visuals. You might say, "At this point, let's put the handouts away and really focus here on the whiteboard. This part is complicated, and you'll need to follow what I'm doing." You can inject a little humor to lighten the mood by saying, "There'll be a quiz right after the talk, so you'll need to pay attention!" That won't be so funny, however, if you actually do have a quiz planned.

When your topic is a complicated one and it's important that your audience be at a relatively high level of understanding of the subject in order to receive your message, an advance mailing is both considerate and intelligent. This, of course, only works when you know exactly who your audience is. If the materials are an essential element of participation in your presentation, you should have extra copies on hand, because people have a tendency to lose or forget things, especially if it is an early morning meeting or if they have had to rush to get there. If you are planning a surprise for your audience, however, don't include it in an advance packet.

COPIES OF THE SPEECH

When certain people have something important to say, others want to keep those words handy for future reference. Politicians, leaders of business and industry, presidents of companies and universities, research scientists, and religious leaders often make copies of their speeches available to the press, or their constituencies, employees, staffs, or fans. The speech is typed in a standard format (not the triple-spaced, all-caps format that the speaker uses when he or she gives the address) and photocopied for distribution. Sometimes the speech, especially if it's a particularly long or weighty one, will be covered with an appropriate cover of heavy, colored stock, and then bound.

If you are uncomfortable telling your audience that copies of your speech will be available to those who are interested, ask the person who introduces you to give the audience that information. It is sometimes useful to have your second or an assistant hand small postcards with a request for a copy of the speech to each participant before they take their seats. (The postcard should probably include postage.) Then participants who want a copy can simply add their name and address to the card and hand it back to the assistant as they leave, or mail it back when they get a chance.

It is rarely appropriate to hand out copies of a speech to the audience in advance. It's better that they watch and hear you rather than read along. However, advance copies are frequently given to the media in advance so that they are more likely to report it in a timely manner and less likely to get things wrong. (See Chapter 10 for more about dealing with the media.)

High-ranking politicians will frequently distribute copies of a speech in advance to key supporters who may be asked to make comments to the media immediately following the speech. If they have had time to read it thoroughly and to digest the information, they are better able to say supportive things about the talk.

FEEDBACK FORMS

Just about every training session I've ever attended concluded with a feedback form. The forms, which often contain no more than five or six questions, but sometimes are several pages long, are designed to help the presentation organizers evaluate the presenter and the material presented. Sometimes this tool for information gathering is subsequently used to determine the effectiveness of the presenter and his program and to help organizers decide whether the event is worth repeating.

In addition, feedback is valuable for the presenter himself and should not be limited to training sessions. If you will be giving the same or a similar presentation a number of times, you may find it helpful to know the previous audience's perception of your performance. By obtaining answers to some simple questions, you'll get some idea of how effective you have been.

A questionnaire is more reliable than just knowing how many people left or fell asleep during your talk, how much yawning or rustling of papers there was, or how many and what types of questions people asked. Because most people will make an effort to be courteous, you could give a terrible presentation and not know it from the polite applause and gracious reactions of your well-mannered audience.

By supplying your audience with a simple, anonymous feedback form that they can mail or hand in at their own convenience, you may find out some difficult truths. Or you may be delighted to find out that your audience really heard what you had to say. Either way, it's helpful to know.

Your host might ask the audience to take a moment to fill out a brief form, or you might make the pitch by saying, in your opening or closing remarks, "Before we leave this afternoon, I'd appreciate it if you could take a minute or two to answer a couple of questions. Your input is important to me."

You might ask these questions:

- On a scale of 1 to 6 (with 1 being the highest), how would rate the presentation overall? the content? the presenter? the visuals?
- If you were to give the presenter advice on improving the presentation, what two things would you recommend?
- What key points do you remember most?
- What aspects of the topic did the presenter leave out that might have been of interest to you?
- Why did you attend?

ON-THE-SPOT HANDOUTS

There are presentation situations in which the final results depend on the level and quality of audience participation. Such situations are often brainstorming or strategy sessions guided by a facilitator or leader. Frequently such meetings include the use of visuals, including lists, mind maps, configurations, and other solutions, created on the spot with a computer and a large screen. The final results or, if important, the route to the results as displayed on the computer screen will be valuable to the participants. These results can be generated by a printer linked to the facilitator's computer; they can be compiled and collated into neat packets for each person to take away with them.

Eight

The Personal You

Surely whoever speaks to me in the right voice,
him or her I shall follow.

> —WALT WHITMAN

It's already been established. No one is more qualified than you are to talk about the subject at hand. You know your audience as well as you know your own family members. Your visuals have been professionally prepared, and all of the logistical considerations have been expertly handled. The presentation is a go.

But, wait. There's more to it.

We're all a little insecure about how others see us. In this chapter, we'll look at how you can put your best foot forward (and that's a well-polished shoe your foot is in!) to make the best possible impression. You'll find specific measures you can take to improve your speaking voice, along with tips on making the personal you a personable and presentable you.

LISTEN TO YOURSELF

The quality of your voice is nearly as important as your message. If a voice is irritating, offensive, high-pitched, nasal, whining, strongly accented, or off-putting in any way, it will distract your audience from the key points of the presentation. A voice that is forced or too loud will sound strident, even aggressive. And if a voice is too soft, the audience won't get the point of the presentation because they won't even hear it.

The only way to know how your voice sounds to others is to hear it for yourself. However, when you speak, you don't hear how your voice *truly* sounds. That's because your ears pick up your voice though a sort of filter made up of the vibrations of sound waves against your facial bones and through the hollows of your sinuses.

The best way to get an accurate sense of your voice quality is to listen to a tape recording. You can use any kind of tape recorder, but be sure to use a high-quality tape so the recording is as accurate and lifelike as possible.

Read a letter, newspaper article, book passage, or prepared speech into the recorder, and then play it back. If you haven't heard yourself before, you'll probably be surprised by your own voice. I was, the first time I heard my taped message on an answering machine.

If you have the time, ask a few friends of the same sex to record the same passage after your segment on the tape. Then analyze the different voices, including your own. How would you describe them? Resonant, strong, and vibrant? Or wispy, fragile, and young? Refined or course? Harsh or soothing?

A well-modulated, low-pitched, resonant, sustained voice is what a presenter needs in order to reach the audience effectively. To achieve that kind of voice, it helps to understand how your voice works.

Hal Persons, who teaches theatrical performance skills to executives, explains in *The How-to of Great Speaking* that the voice starts from the lungs as a column of air. When this column of air reaches the vocal cords, the vocal cords vibrate, creating sound. The sound travels to the mouth where the lips, tongue, and teeth form it into vowels and consonants, which become words. Many people use their throats to increase the volume of their voices, resulting in a forced sound. This can actually injure the throat and cause the formation of nodes, which, in the worst cases, must be surgically removed.

The proper way to turn up the volume of your voice is with breath support. Shouting isn't the answer. However, by breathing from your diaphragm, you can increase the level of sound that comes from your vocal cords without strain, and without sounding forced or strident. (See the section in this chapter entitled "Talking from Way Down" to learn how to support your speech with deep breaths from your abdomen.)

Tone, Pitch, and Inflection

A major obstacle to effective speech is high pitch. Unfortunately, many women have a particular problem with voice pitch that can make even the most knowledgeable, powerful, effective executive sound unsure, immature, or childlike.

Far too many people, and this again is more often a problem for women, raise the inflection of their voices inappropriately at the end of a declarative sentence. For example, read the following proposal out loud:

The board should consider a 6 percent across-the-board salary increase for support staff.

Now read the same sentence, but this time with the words in bold raised in the form of a question:

*The board should consider a 6 percent across-the-board salary increase for **support staff**.*

Instead of making a strong argument for raising salaries, the speaker sabotaged his or her effectiveness and severely weakened the proposal. The inflection of the voice at the end of the sentence is the culprit. An upward inflection suggests a question to the listener; a lowered inflection says, "This is a fact."

Working on pitch is a little more challenging. In her book *BusinessSpeak*, Suzette Haden Elgin, PhD, offers a step-by-step do-it-yourself plan for improving the tone and pitch of your speaking voice. With her technique, called Simultaneous Modeling, you can train your own voice by modeling it after that of an actor or newscaster.

She points out that television journalist Diane Sawyer's voice offers an excellent female model and that news anchor Peter Jennings's voice is a good choice for men. Other excellent models include the voices of Candice Bergen (when she's not shrieking), Jane Fonda, Bernard Shaw (from CNN), Mike Wallace, Glenn Close, Peter Graves, and Dan Rather. Most of the on-air personalities at National Public Radio have wonderful speaking voices too.

In Dr. Elgin's program, which includes a series of twenty-minute sessions done at least three times a week, you speak along with a tape recording of a voice you are trying to model. She claims that with diligent practice you can dramatically improve the quality of your voice, though she cautions that this process can take six months, a year, or longer.

A raised pitch makes the speaker sound insecure, unsure, shrill, or even angry; a lowered pitch, especially at the end of a sentence or for emphasis, adds strength and conviction to a statement. Read the following sentence with a high-pitched tone at the end:

Forty-two percent of the county's residents over the age of eighteen are not registered to vote.

Now read it in a lower pitch, and even lower for the words in bold print:

*Forty-two percent of the county's residents over the age of eighteen **are not registered to vote.***

See how much more important those words are when they are delivered in a lower-pitched voice!

If you find it difficult to lower the pitch of your voice, make an effort to relax your neck and throat muscles. Try humming a low monotone. Then groan or moan from your chest. You can moan, hum, and groan in the shower or in the car where you won't have an audience. If you do these exercises at home, let your family know what you're doing, or they may become alarmed!

Another trick for lowering the pitch of your voice is to open your mouth a little wider when you speak. Just be sure you don't look like you're gulping for air.

To practice speaking in a lower pitch, select a quotation and repeat it with an increasingly lower pitch. Just for fun, try one of these:

- "Good night and good luck." (Edward R. Murrow)
- "As I grow older and older and totter toward the tomb, I find that I care less and less who goes to bed with whom." (Dorothy Sayers)
- "Parody is homage gone sour." (Brendan Gill)
- "Character consists of what you do on the third and fourth tries." (James Michener)
- "An atheist is a man who has no invisible means of support." (Bishop Fulton Sheen)

Practice moving the pitch around, using a lower pitch at different points in the quotation. Isn't it amazing how you can change the tone of what you are saying just by changing the pitch?

Try adjusting your volume too, and see what happens. Sometimes you will create greater emphasis by lowering the volume of your voice—like speaking in a stage whisper. In the right circumstances, this is an especially strong attention grabber.

Hal Persons suggests these actor's exercises for improving your speaking voice:

- Drop your chin to your chest, then roll your head first toward your right shoulder, and then toward your left, five times.
- Make a big yawn, five times.
- Whisper a poem or long quotation.
- Hum to a count of five, breathe, and repeat.

Here are a few more tips for improving your speaking voice:

- Avoid hot or cold liquids just before speaking. Sip cool (not iced) water during your presentation.
- Avoid dairy products before speaking. They can make your throat feel thick.
- Learn how to relax the muscles in your throat and neck.
- Stand up straight. Balance your weight evenly on both feet.
- Breathe normally. Don't hyperventilate.
- Avoid wearing shirts, blouses, ties, or jewelry that are too tight around the neck.
- Don't clear your throat repeatedly. It can cause hoarseness.

(See Chapter 4 for helpful ideas on delivery, including vocal variety, pace, body language, language, posture, enunciation, and style.)

TALKING FROM WAY DOWN HERE

Actors, singers, and other performers who rely on their voices learn to breathe differently in order to add strength and projection to their voices. They breathe from the diaphragm, the large muscle that lies below the rib cage. You can feel your diaphragm if you put your hand just below your rib cage and just above your navel and breath deeply. You can exercise your diaphragm by blowing into a balloon, or pretending to, and then inhaling slowly.

Use your abdominal muscles, keeping them taut and pulled in. Repeat as many times as you can without getting dizzy. You'll know that you are using your diaphragm when your stomach extends when you speak; if it contracts, then you're not using it. Exercising the abdominals, a great idea for fitness, is also a big plus for your voice.

Gena Ciccone, a young voice and theater student, practices the following exercises to increase her breath support for singing and acting:

- Lie on your back on the floor with a few large books on your abdomen. While taking deep breaths, try to raise the books. Lower them as you exhale.
- With the books still on your stomach, repeat a phrase, quotation, or nursery rhyme while pressing on the books. This forces the air from your diaphragm up into your mouth.
- Push against your abdomen while you speak so that your feel the air moving upward. Do this while standing.
- Expand your abdomen when you inhale. Contract it when you exhale.

If you practice these exercises for a few months before your presentation, you should be able to breathe from the diaphragm, thus improving your speaking voice and giving it more volume and depth.

HINTS ON DELIVERY

In the July 1996 issue of *Performance Improvement* (Vol. 35, No. 6), Peter J. Dean, Julee K. Brooke, and Linda B. Shields created a set of instructions for perfecting a speaker's delivery. Their advice is easy to understand and follow:

Increase your believability or credibility—
- Increase your vocal intensity.
- Inflect your voice downward.
- Speak at a slower rate.

Inspire your audience—
- Use up and down inflections often (but don't use a singsong pattern).
- Watch your pace and timing—use thoughtful pauses.
- Add enthusiasm to your tone.

Get rid of the jitters—
- Breathe normally.
- Articulate clearly.
- Monitor your pitch to keep it from rising.

Avoid a monotone—
- Vary your pitch.
- Vary intensity and loudness.
- Inflect up or down.
- Vary your pace and timing.

Get rid of the "ums" and "ahs"—
- Prepare thoroughly.
- Practice your talk.

- Review tape- or video-recorded practice sessions.
- Use a pause instead of an "um."

Improve your diction—
- Enunciate clearly.
- Use proper pronunciation.
- Practice often.

Eliminate vocal strain—
- Practice proper breathing.
- Open your mouth and nasal passages for resonance.
- Practice speaking more softly.

PROFESSIONAL TRAINING

If you aren't the type to follow a self-training schedule, if you aren't making much progress, if your voice is particularly poor, or if your accent is uncomfortably strong, you may want to consider professional voice coaching—especially if you will be spending a good deal of time making presentations. You can expect some improvement in the quality of your voice after several sessions, if you are willing to conscientiously practice the training techniques.

To find a qualified voice teacher, ask for referrals from a college or university speech or theater department, the chamber of commerce, a local Toastmaster's Club, a community theater group, or a church choir director. Some speech therapists also do voice coaching. Though voice training with a professional is a somewhat expensive undertaking, your accountant will most likely consider the fees a valid business expense.

TRY TOASTMASTERS

It's possible to get training for speech-making and pre-senting through participation in a Toastmaster's Club. This international not-for-profit organization, founded in 1924 in Santa Ana, California, has about 8,000 corporate and community clubs in fifty countries. Companies like Coca-Cola, CitiBank, Eastman Kodak, IBM, Kraft, Apple Computers, and Rockwell International have used the Toastmaster's program for improving sales presentations and developing skills for internal speakers' bureau members. Toastmaster club meetings typically include opportunities for members to give impromptu and prepared speeches, followed by evaluation sessions with feedback on strengths and weaknesses of the presentation along with a critique of the evaluation.

To find a Toastmaster's Club in your community, visit their Web site at www.toastmasters.org or call their international headquarters at (714) 858-8255.

WHAT TO WEAR

Once you know your audience (see Chapter 1) and you've established what type of presentation to make (Chapter 2), you can decide what to wear when you present. If you know your audience well, you should have a pretty good idea of what they expect from you. In order for your audience to have confidence in you, your presentation wardrobe should reflect how your audience expects you to dress.

So, if you are giving a presentation to municipal government officials on a bond issue, dress the way your audience thinks a financial expert should. If your audience is expecting an artistic flair from you, for example, when you present an advertising campaign, don't disappoint them by dressing like a banker.

In ordinary business situations, a conservative, well-cut suit with a neatly pressed shirt or blouse is always appropriate for men and women presenters. And a convenient rule for planning your presentation wardrobe is to dress just slightly more formally than your audience.

Women have a great deal more variety in their choices for presentation wear; they are no longer restricted to man-tailored suits. If you like to wear dresses, and they look good on you, then wear a dress. Be sure to get an objective opinion about how the dress looks (coming and, especially, going). A dress with matching jacket is a good choice. Avoid sleeveless dresses unless it's extremely hot *and* you have very shapely upper arms.

There are two schools of thought when it comes to identifying suitable clothing colors for a business presenter. The conservative view, espoused by the editors of *The Executive's Guide to Successful Presentations*, is that gray and blue are the most appropriate suit colors for both men and women and should be worn with pale blue, burgundy, or gray ties or scarves.

Dorothy Sarnoff thinks there's room for much more diversity. She is the founder and chairman of Speech Dynamics and has advised clients such as Senators Bob Dole and Lloyd Bentsen, along with prime ministers, authors, and television newscasters. In her book *Never Be Nervous Again*, Ms. Sarnoff recommends that her clients wear standout colors such as red, royal blue, kelly green, and even hot pink and turquoise. Men should wear pink, blue, mauve, or even yellow shirts, with ties in complementary colors. She says, "When you're presenting why not be the center of attention? Have your color enter the room and claim attention with you."

I agree with Ms. Sarnoff. Strong colors are uplifting and eye-catching. And if the suit, dress, shirt, or tie is conservatively styled, the color is not a bit distracting. If you decide to wear vibrant colors, be sure to select those that compliment your eye and hair color and skin tones.

But what about presentations that fall outside the category of "business"? In these situations, the presenters' dress should be directly connected to the audience and the type of presentation they are expecting. For example, a golf pro should wear sports clothes when giving a presentation on improving one's swing. An automotive engineer should probably wear coveralls when doing a hands-on presentation on repair techniques for mechanics.

If your company, department, or client has asked you to present at an off-site venue in a nonbusiness setting, for example, a ski or beach resort, dude ranch, or mountain retreat, you should dress for the setting. But keep in the mind the rule about being just slightly more formal than your audience. For example, if the venue is a golf resort and your audience is dressed in polo shirts and Bermuda shorts, you should wear casual slacks, an open-necked shirt, and a casual blazer, if you are a man; a woman might select a skirt and blouse or a cotton dress with a short-sleeved jacket.

A few more hints on what to wear:

- Cuff links that show just below a jacket sleeve are the new power statement for men—but only when they're of good quality. Avoid flash.
- Bold earrings enliven a women's face and draw the audience's attention to her face.
- A colorful scarf, an interesting necklace, or a nice pin at the shoulder also draws attention to a speaker's face and can help keep an audience focused.

WHAT NOT TO WEAR

Dorothy Sarnoff warns women that wearing pants will diminish their effectiveness as presenters, that "brown is down," and that white shirts don't do it anymore. White socks are a no-no in nearly any circumstance, unless you are a tennis pro presenting a new line of racquets.

Because you want to make a positive impression on your audience, whatever the purpose of your presentation, your clothing should never be wrinkled, ripped, soiled, missing buttons, or obviously out of date. Your shoes should be shined and well heeled. Your stockings should be run-free. The lining of your coat or jacket shouldn't hang below the hem. For women, slips and bra straps should remain out of sight (as should your cleavage).

Other sartorial pitfalls include vests (they tend to make people look overweight), double-breasted suits (they only work well on the very slim), bow ties (they are appropriate only if "absent-minded professor" is the image you are trying to create), and anything that's too big or too small.

Though it's entirely unfair, overweight people have a harder time commanding respect, credibility, and authority. If you are carrying a few extra pounds, you need to be especially careful to select clothing that doesn't accentuate your weight problem. Be sure your shirts and blouses aren't strained at the buttons. And give yourself plenty of room across the stomach and the derriere. Check your appearance in a full-length mirror, and get an objective opinion on how you look from the rear, well in advance—just in case you need to do some quick shopping.

If you wear the wrong clothes, your audience will find it distracting. And no matter how qualified you are, ill-fitting, inappropriate clothes will make you look insecure, incompetent, unsophisticated, and sloppy.

YOUR HANDS

You can tell a great deal about a person just by looking at his or her hands. Chipped, uneven fingernails bespeak a person with low self-esteem. Long red talons and nails decorated with patterns or rhinestones (yes, some women actually do that!) shriek "lightweight."

A presenter should have clean, well-manicured hands. But then so should everyone.

It is important that your hands do not distract the audience. You don't want people wondering, for example, what you do in your spare time that makes your hands look so beat up. And you don't want them thinking, "How can she get anything done with so many rings on her fingers?"

Your hands can be an asset when you speak if you use them eloquently, because they reinforce your points and make emphasis. (See Chapter 5 for tips on how to use your hands to improve your delivery.)

Here are a few hints regarding hands:

- Manicure your nails the day before your presentation. Colored nails look great on most women, but make sure they aren't overly long or pointed. Men should forgo the polish unless it's customary among audience members.
- Two or three rings are fine for women, especially those with nice hands. Men should stick with one ring, or two at the most. Some people find diamonds or other gemstones on men distracting.
- Unless you are a confident, experienced speaker and it's part of your style, keep your hands out of your pockets while you speak. And avoid jingling change in your pockets. That makes you look nervous and is very distracting.
- If your hands are trembling, hold on to the sides of the podium, but do so lightly. You don't want to look like you are holding on for dear life. If there is no lectern, you can hold your notes gently or clasp your hands together loosely and hold them at your waist. Just be careful not to wring them. That's an awful sight.
- Avoid twisting the rings on your fingers. It's another sign of nervousness.
- Make sure your hands aren't clenched in a fist. The tightened muscles can exacerbate your nervousness.
- Don't shred a tissue, unbend a paper clip, twist a straw, or mutilate any other object while you speak. It makes a mess and makes you look as terrified as you feel.

- If you tend to sweat, keep a clean, white pocket handkerchief in your pocket or on the lectern shelf and feel free to dab at your face from time to time. This will be less distracting for the audience than watching drops of sweat drip from your chin and nose.

YOUR HAIR

How you wear your hair is very personal, but it's also part of the package that is you. So your hair must meet the same high standards as your dress, your voice, and your delivery style.

Here are a few pointers:

- Never try a new hairstyle or color just before a presentation; if you hate it, you'll be self-conscious and that will show.
- Don't get your hair cut less than three days from your presentation date.
- Don't allow hair to cover your eyebrows. You need to show your audience as much facial expression as possible.
- If you have dandruff, work on getting rid of it. Snowy shoulders are distracting, particularly when your audience is seated close to you.
- If your hair is unruly, use some spray to keep it in place. This goes for men as well as women.
- If you have worn the same hairstyle for years, get an objective opinion about it. It may be time for an update.
- Overly long hair on older women can be unflattering. Pony tails on men can be distracting too. Just keep your audience in mind.
- If age is an issue in your field, give serious thought to coloring the gray in your hair and beard.
- Speaking of beards—keep yours neatly trimmed and the mustache well away from your lips.

Nine

Special Situations

Rarely is life totally predictable. From time to time we are called on to deal with special situations. This chapter, aptly entitled "Special Situations," looks at those times.

For example, you may be asked to make an impromptu presentation. Or you may be asked at the last minute to introduce a presenter. At another time, you may be invited to address your daughter's class about what it is you do between 9 and 5. Perhaps the activities director at a local retirement community will corner you and shame you into speaking at her next current events club meeting. Or you may find yourself addressing people with disabilities, who may need some assistance in receiving your message.

This chapter includes some pointers on how you can be effective in situations that may not fall within your normal frame of reference.

IMPROMPTU SITUATIONS

The best impromptu speeches are the ones written well in advance.

—RUTH GORDON

Always expect the unexpected. There may be times when, for example, a speaker doesn't show up and you'll be called on to deliver some relevant remarks. Or you may be at a meeting and hear your boss or a colleague say, "Well, Pat, you've been working on Project Rebound since the beginning. What are your thoughts on the target dates?"—and you'll have no choice but to oblige.

And sometimes it's just appropriate for you to speak "off the cuff." (By the way, the expression "off the cuff" came from the idea of writing notes to oneself on the removable cuff of one's shirt, back in the days when the removable collars and cuffs of shirts were laundered more often than the shirts themselves.)

If you genuinely feel unprepared to speak, it's probably better to be honest about it rather than to risk making a serious error. But if, in fact, you are asked to make an impromptu presentation related to your expertise, experience, or knowledge, accept the honor and go ahead.

Janet Stone and Jane Bachner, the authors of *Speaking Up, A Book for Every Woman Who Wants to Speak Effectively*, suggest that an impromptu speaker think of his or her conclusion first, with the idea that this will provide structure for the impromptu presentation and the rest will fall into place. I think it's good advice.

When faced with an impromptu situation, ask for a minute to collect your thoughts. Focus on a conclusion, decide on one or two key points, jot them down, and pencil in a few details. Try to formulate a mini-outline, a shorter version of what you would do if you had been given plenty of time to prepare for a regular presentation. Remember to have an opener, a middle (chunked with perhaps three key points), and a close. (See Chapter 3 for more details.)

Don't apologize for not having a prepared presentation. After all, this just landed in your lap and everyone knows it. You should start out with something like "You're right Leslie, I have been involved with Project Rebound from day one, and it's been a challenge for the entire team right from the start. The target dates for our introduction are probably too optimistic . . ." That's the opener—short and to the point.

Next, give a few good reasons why the target date is too optimistic. Then close with a more realistic date, recommendations for speeding up the process, or a suggestion for changing the project to fit the schedule. Avoid rambling on; by keeping it short you are more likely to provide an organized, intelligent presentation.

At the end of an impromptu prevention, you should ask if anyone has questions. You might offer to make a more detailed presentation on the subject at a future date when you will have had adequate time to prepare a more in-depth report.

INTRODUCTIONS

On occasion you may be asked to introduce a presenter. If you have some experience as a presenter yourself, you shouldn't have any difficulty in making an introduction. You simply have to follow the Golden Rule and do unto other presenters as you would have them do unto you.

Even if you know the presenter, ask for a copy of a curriculum vitae or resume and look it over carefully. Be sure you know how to correctly pronounce his or her name. Ask the presenter to highlight some of the curriculum vitae entries that are of particular importance or that are most applicable to the presentation situation.

Keep the introduction short. After all, the presenter is the main event, not your prelude. Milo O. Frank, the author of *How to Get Your Point Across in 30 Seconds or Less*, suggests that an introduction that is longer than thirty seconds is not an introduction at all; it's a speech! He has a point, but I think most speakers deserve a little more than thirty seconds of introduction. You can allow up to about two minutes, especially if the presenter is extremely well known, has a long list of credentials, or is giving a long presentation. But any longer than two minutes and your audience may start thinking, "Let's get this show on the road." You should introduce a short presentation, say ten minutes or so, succinctly—Milo Frank's thirty-second rule certainly applies to those situations.

Your goal in making an introduction is to warm the audience and prepare them to accept the presenter. You can do this by relating significant highlights of the presenters credentials, relevant educational or professional information, recent accomplishments, and notable awards. Then tell the audience what the presenter will be talking about. If the talk has a title, use it. If not, explain what the presentation is about, using a very brief description: "This morning, Marcia Taylor will lead us through the recent changes in federal regulations for managed care companies." Or "Jason Marks, of Jazzy Jeans, will introduce us to the fall line of teen jeans."

In *Speaking Up*, Janet Stone and Jane Bachner explore the rather complicated psychology of introducing a speaker. They point out that an introduction can shape the attitude of the audience. For example, if the presentation is about a topic that is controversial, the person who makes the introduction can prime the audience to be more or less receptive to the message. The introduction can prepare the audience for bad news; it can stimulate negative expectations or introduce a positive tone. You should do your best to make a positive introduction, one that will invite a receptive, respectful response from the audience. If your attitude toward the presenter is hostile, perhaps you should rethink your role. Will your own agenda jeopardize the success of the presentation?

Sometimes it's appropriate to introduce a speaker by using an amusing anecdote, as long as it doesn't make fun of the speaker in any way. The anecdote may come from a personal experience you share with the presenter, or he or she may provide you with a story. Just keep it short.

Also, always run through your introduction with the speaker to avoid relating a story the presenter plans to use during the talk. If the presenter's dog ate her notes an hour before she was scheduled to speak, it might make a funny intro. But if she had planned to use that amusing tidbit in her opener, she'll be thrown off balance to hear it seconds before she faces the audience.

You should also avoid using superlatives and hype when making an introduction. And never say, "You're going to be amazed by what she has to say." (What if they're not?) Also avoid saying, "She is the best in her field"—unless she actually is!

TOASTS

One definition of a toast is "a proposal to drink to someone or something, or a speech given before the taking of such a drink." At some point in your personal or professional life, you will probably be called on to make a toast to honor a relative, colleague, or friend, to praise the successful launch of a project or product, or to bid farewell or to welcome.

In most cases, you'll have plenty of time to think of just the right toast. Weddings, retirement dinners, award ceremonies, and gala events usually have several months lead time. There are also plenty of books with prepared toasts from which to choose. But you may want to write your own. The key to a successful toast is to keep it very short, pithy, and sincere.

Many of the best-known toasts are attributed to the Irish, for example, "May your death give nobody pleasure!" and "May you be in heaven an hour before the devil knows you're dead."

Here are some additional well-known toasts from which to chose or to use as models for creating your own:

> "May we have a few real friends rather than a thousand acquaintances."

> "To your good health, old friend, may you live for a thousand years, and I be there to count them."—Robert Smith Surtees

> "May harmony fill our hearts, not merely charm our ears."

> "Here's to those of us who are friends, and let the rest of the world make its own arrangements."

> "Here's to your good health, and your family's good health, and may you live long and prosper."—Washington Irving, from *Rip Van Winkle*

> "May the work that you have be the play that you love."

> "Here's to success, which can set its roots deep only through soil enriched by countless failures."

"To the dignity of labor and the benefit of its ends."

"May you live all the days of your life!"—Jonathan Swift

"To peace and friendship among all people."—Jimmy Carter

"Let us toast the fools; but for them the rest of us could not succeed."—Mark Twain

GROUPS AND PANELS

There are many occasions on which several presenters share the stage. An organization's annual meeting often includes a series of speakers or presenters. Sometimes panel discussions are scheduled. And in some cases, especially in sales situations, a collaborative group makes the presentation.

When you are one of several speakers seated on the stage or at the head table, it's only common courtesy to sit quietly and listen to what the others have to say. Try not to yawn, and for heaven's sake don't glance at your watch. Look like you care about what is being said even if you don't. When it's your turn, perhaps the other speakers will do the same for you.

In many multiple-speaker situations, the host or master of ceremonies will go to the podium after each speaker to introduce the next one. But from time to time you may run into a circumstance in which each speaker introduces the next. Be sure to find out in advance how the introductions will be handled. You should prepare your own introduction—something short, no more than thirty seconds—to give to the speaker scheduled before you. He or she will appreciate not having one more thing to think about, and you'll be introduced in a way you consider to be appropriate.

A panel discussion is a different category of presentation. In most cases, the panelists sit at a head table or at a table on the stage. In large venues, each panelists should have a microphone placed in front of him. A moderator is usually seated with the panelists or sometimes stands at a podium nearby. Usually the moderator serves as the link between the audience and the panelists. She is most often the person who introduces the panelists and frequently the one who takes questions from the audience, sometimes assigning them to specific panelists.

Being on a panel can be a wonderful experience. For those who suffer from stage fright, a person sitting close by can be a comfort. And it can be invigorating to share ideas with other experts.

But there can be drawbacks. If the moderator hasn't spelled out the ground rules by allotting each panelist a specific amount of time (or if she isn't a strong person or doesn't see a problem), you and the other panelists may have to relinquish most of the time to an egomaniac or time hog who thinks his or her words are more important than anyone else's. It's not easy to rectify such a situation while it's happening. If you interrupt, you may appear rude. But if things get really out of hand, you should certainly try to get your thoughts in. You might try to say, "I'd like to interject . . ." or "If I might add this thought . . ." or "Excuse me, Bob, there's an additional point to make on that issue . . ." And remember, you can disagree with the other panelists. That's part of the fun and interest of a panel discussion.

Presenting with a collaborative group is yet another special situation in which you may find yourself involved. Often sales efforts are done collaboratively. Architectural firms often send a team to present the plans for a major design project. Advertising agencies frequently send out a whole group when they present proposals for an ad campaign. Investment banking firms, insurance companies, design studios, and myriad other businesses regularly send in their big guns to present their plans, because often there is no one person who is expert in every aspect of the project.

Working on a collaborative presentation is tricky. But with good planning, it can be a rewarding experience. The key to success in a collaborative effort is to spell out everyone's responsibilities right from the start. Someone should serve as the team leader, someone who has to have the authority and the ability to make decisions and to assign tasks. If the group does not include a senior member, the team should assign a coordinator and give that person what she needs to keep the team on task

Scott Ober, the author of *Contemporary Business Communication*, points out that the division of duties should be made based on each member's strengths. One person may be a research wiz, so the data collection tasks should go to him, though he may need help from other members of the team. Another may be more able to handle the visuals, while someone else's strong suit might be logistics. Others in the group may be strong presenters; others might prefer to stay in the background.

Ober suggests that early in the effort a collaborative team should agree on the format, tone, and style of the presentation. The members should have discussions about how a Q&A session should be handled and how they should dress. He also thinks full-scale rehearsals (videotaped for analysis and critique) are a good idea.

In order for a collaborative presentation to be successful, every member of the team has to "buy into" the project and share the responsibilities and workload. There's no room for personality conflicts, ego trips, or laziness. If the presentation is a success, each team member, even those who don't actually speak during the event, should be publicly acknowledged.

A word about sitting at a table on stage: If the table isn't skirted, remember that the audience is looking up at you from slightly below and that they have a view of your legs and feet. This is not a good time to wear a very short skirt or trousers that are too short. Your shoes should be polished. And if you are wearing older shoes, check to see that there aren't any holes in the soles.

While you shouldn't be concentrating on your feet, you should keep them in mind. Don't put them up on the rungs of the chair or wrap them around the chair's legs. Keep your legs together as comfortably as possible with your feet flat on the floor or crossed at the ankle. You can lean forward slightly from the waist and rest your wrists on the table. Elbows on the table might also be okay, especially if the other panelists are doing it. But don't hunch over.

Keep your shoulders back and your back straight; it will keep your voice strong, and you'll look more authoritative.

ADDRESSING GOVERNMENT AGENCIES

Comin' as close to the truth as a man can come
without actually gettin' there is comin' pretty
close, but it still ain't the truth.
                                    —TEXAS BIX BINDER

Few of us will be asked to address a congressional committee, the Environmental Protection Agency, or the Food and Drug Administration; but it's not unthinkable that at some point we will appear before a government agency of some sort—municipal councils, school or zoning boards, planning commissions, environmental or architectural review boards, for example. The key to success when making a presentation to a government agency is thorough preparation. You need to know your material inside and out, upside down, and backward. Have the answer to every question that could possibly be asked and be able to site your sources.

It's also wise to be aware that the activities of government agencies, from senate committees to town councils, are followed by the media, whether it's CNN, C-SPAN or the local weekly rag. (See Chapter 10 for more information about working with the media.) And most meetings are recorded in some fashion, sometimes on videotape and often on audiotape, or by a stenographer.

Because what you say before a government agency has the potential to come back to haunt you, you must be absolutely sure that what you say is true and unimpeachable. Don't exaggerate. Never lie. Play it straight.

Brevity, though a virtue for most presentation situations, is not required, nor is it necessarily an advantage, for the presenter addressing a government agency. For some reason bureaucrats and politicians seem to have enormous amounts of stamina when it comes to sitting in meetings and listening to constituents, experts, witnesses, consultants, and other bureaucrats and politicians.

And because they are so often very concerned about covering their posteriors, they want to make sure that every scrap of information is in their hands before they make decisions or act on an issue. In nearly every situation, presenters also provide the agency with all the information in writing.

If your purpose is to inform, just present the facts, every last one of them, and answer questions as they are posed. If, however, you want to persuade the agency, for example the FDA or a senate hearing, on an environmental issue, you will need to use all of the persuasive techniques you possess. (See Chapter 3 for more information about persuasive presentations.) If you are scheduled to appear before a state or federal agency, you should look into all the legal ramifications and follow the instructions of your contact at the agency.

To prepare yourself for the appearance, try watching the C-SPAN coverage of a hearing or meeting. How do the participants conduct themselves? Notice how some people seem to slouch before the microphone, leaning on their elbows. It's not particularly attractive. In fact, it's pretty negative body language—not the kind of personal style that will make the speaker appear credible and authoritative.

A better position is to sit with your back straight and your hands folded on the table in front of you. Have someone adjust the microphone so you don't have to lean forward or stretch to speak into it. (See the section on podiums and microphones in Chapter 6.) Of course you'll be able to consult your notes. Keep them in a neat folder—a leather or vinyl one will look professional.

Allow yourself plenty of time to think about your answers—this isn't the same kind of situation you'll encounter in a normal Q&A session after a talk. And speak clearly and succinctly. Remember that even the most experienced presenters are often intimidated by this kind of experience.

OLDER PEOPLE

Older people are consumers with considerable political clout, along with more discretionary time than most younger folk. They often find themselves being addressed by political candidates vowing to look after their interests, by bureaucrats attempting to explain changes in Medicare or Social Security, and by health experts promoting exercise and nutrition concepts.

Activities directors at retirement communities and continuing care facilities pride themselves on scheduling a seemingly endless stream of talks, workshops, lectures, seminars, and presentations. These activities provide residents with interesting and engaging things to do with their copious free time.

As the baby-boomer population ages, the number of presentations made to the older demographic cohort will increase. And chances are you will at some time be called on to make a presentation to this audience.

An audience of retired teachers differs from an audience of working teachers in that the older audience is more likely to have some difficulties in hearing a presenter (see anecdote). They may not see your visuals as clearly. They may be more likely to nod off during a talk. And their attention spans may be somewhat shorter than those of younger people.

Other than these few differences, audiences composed of older people are just as interested or disinterested in what you have to say as any other group. Once you have accounted for hearing deficits and visual impairments, you are just as likely to wow them as not, based on your presentation style and content.

Here are a few tips that may help you reach an older audience:

- Never, ever talk down to your audience. Older people get their fill of patronizing behavior and will not respond positively to someone who uses it.
- Always use electronic amplification when addressing a group of older adults. Most venues used frequently by groups of senior citizens will have equipment available, but don't make that assumption. Ask the appropriate

logistical questions, and follow up to ensure that the equipment will be in place. Or take your own.

- Use oversized type and plenty of contrast for your visuals.
- Incorporate appropriate humor.
- Keep the talk relatively short. Many older people have trouble sitting in one position for long periods of time. If they start to feel uncomfortable, need to use the bathroom, or are worrying about being late for lunch, you've lost them.

After presenting a slide lecture on English gardens to a local garden club, I was approached by an elderly member of the audience; she had an even older woman on her arm. She told me that while she enjoyed looking at my pictures, she hadn't heard a word I said. This was the same woman who, after the first minute or so of my presentation, had asked me to speak up. I had encouraged her, and anyone else in the audience who had trouble hearing me, to move up to the front of the room where there were several empty seats. She and her companion had declined to move, and I had done my best to make my voice louder. Obviously I had failed to make it loud enough. When I asked her why she hadn't moved to the front, she pointed to her friend and said, "Addy has trouble getting around and I couldn't leave her."

Because many of the garden club members were older people, I should have expected that some of them would have difficulty hearing. I should have insisted on some kind of amplification so my audience could hear what I had to say.

CHILDREN

For some presenters, working with kids is a pleasure. Others feel nothing but pain. You may never have to address a group of children. It's not something I would choose to do. And I've only had to do it a few times. Once I was asked to participate in a career day at our local high school and give a short presentation about the field of public relations.

The setting was informal—a group of about a dozen students, a teacher, and me sitting at desks moved into a circle. I gave a brief description of what public relations is all about, including a couple of what I thought to be amusing anecdotes. I got absolutely no reaction—nothing—but blank, disinterested stares. How could I have failed so miserably? I didn't think I could possibly be that boring.

Mercifully, the bell rang, indicating the end of the session, and the kids escaped. I begged the teacher to tell me what I had done wrong. She looked amused and explained to me that the children in the group were there because they had to be. They hadn't elected to learn about public relations. Essentially, they were there under duress. Had I known this beforehand, I would never have agreed to participate.

But here's an entirely different scenario with essentially the same high school audience. A former drug addict and gang member addressed an assembly on the dangers of illegal drug use. He recounted his own experiences in graphic and horrifying detail. One youngster left the room in tears; another fainted. The remaining one hundred or so were riveted to every word he uttered. That afternoon, my daughter who was a member of that audience, recounted his entire presentation, just about word for word. This former druggie, ex-con was able to reach her and the other kids in the audience with his frightening message. Why?

Because he knew his audience. He had one key point. And he believed passionately in his message.

Most of us won't be able to reach children as effectively as the antidrug speaker, but we still have valuable information, ideas, and convictions to share with them. If you are offered the opportunity to speak to kids, do it. Perhaps they'll learn something. You definitely will.

Here are some tricks to make presenting to kids more pleasant for you and for them:

- Understand that young children need to move around. They can still absorb what you are presenting even though they may fidget and squirm.
- Give the youngest audiences a few seconds of controlled wiggle time before you begin your presentation.
- Keep it short. Ask the teacher or adult in charge how much time is appropriate for the age group you are working with.
- Use as much audience participation as you can. For a fire safety program, for example, have them repeat "stop, drop, and roll" in their loudest voices. If you are presenting the culture of Mexico, encourage the children to speak some words in Spanish. Pretend you can't hear them so they will have to say it louder. If there is adequate space, have them act things out with you.
- Repeat your key points several times, asking the children to "remind" you of what it is you are teaching them.
- If you offer handouts, have enough for every child. Kids will feel left out and cheated even if your handout is only a piece of paper. Don't distribute handouts until after your presentation, unless they are needed for audience participation.
- Add surprises. Yell or sing out suddenly. Bang a drum or ring a bell. Do a cartwheel. It is important to keep the

focus on you, not on a wiggly neighbor or something out-side the window.

- Be silly. Kids love it, and they are more likely to remember your message if they associate it with something fun.
- Ask for their attention if necessary. Sometimes kids will get carried away by the moment and forget where their focus should be. At some point you may need to say, "Girls and boys, I need your attention now." Or "Let's quiet down, please." Keep a friendly tone, but be firm. In some schools, the teacher will raise her hand with fingers forming a V to indicate that it's time to quiet down. Ask if there is a signal familiar to the children in your audience that you can use, should the need arise.
- Be flexible. You may find, minutes into your presentation, that you're not connecting with your young audience. They may be more or less mature than you had expected. They may be at a higher or lower intellectual level than you had planned for. Be prepared to shift gears and alter your program. They may be able to absorb only one of your key points. Select one and hammer that message home with humor and action. Leave the other points for another time.
- Connect your message with something the children can identify with. If your talk is about preventing drunk driving, ask the kids if anyone they know died as a result of a drunk driver. Then ask them how they would feel if they could have prevented that death.

PEOPLE WITH DISABILITIES

Addressing groups of people with visual or hearing impairments requires a few adjustments to your presentation style. An audience composed of the deaf and hearing impaired will probably require an expert in sign language to "translate" your speech. He or she should be supplied with a written copy of your presentation in advance. The audience may also appreciate your text, or an outline. Overheads, blackboard or easel, and video illustrations may be useful. Slides can also be effective, but only if they can be seen without dimming the lights when a signer is working.

Some people with hearing impairments excel at lipreading, and they should have front-row seats reserved for them. You can assist the lipreading process by enunciating clearly, and by applying a strong-colored lipstick or by trimming your mustache. Keep your hands away from your mouth, and be sure your face is not obscured by the podium or a pointer. And never speak while your head is turned away from your audience.

When addressing an audience with visual impairments, you might want to keep in mind some of the same techniques used during a radio presentation. Since the audience can't see you, your voice, and of course your words, must carry the bulk of your message. Speak clearly and succinctly, and use plenty of inflections and vocal variety to take the place of gestures and facial expressions.

If your presentation includes opportunities for questions from your audience, you'll need to devise a method of recognizing those asking questions. Your second or an assistant can circulate in the audience and give a light tap on the shoulder of or speak to the individual to indicate their turn to ask a question. Make sure that the person in charge of setting up chairs for your presentation makes space available for participants in wheelchairs to move through the aisles, should the need arise.

WHEN THE PRESENTER HAS A HEARING IMPAIRMENT

Presenters who have difficulty hearing should not have to give up making presentations. In fact, there are a few modifications they can make to remedy the situation.

If your hearing is less than perfect, you may have trouble judging the level of your own voice. Think about doing a voice check with your second at your presentation venue in advance of your appearance. You may need to raise or lower the volume of your voice, or you may need to employ electronic amplification.

More important is your interaction with the audience. I attended a Master Gardener presentation given by an accomplished botany professor from Penn State whose address was interesting and informative, and I enjoyed it. But at the end, when the class had questions for him, the professor was unable to understand any of them. He just couldn't hear.

Many of the participants left without learning what he no doubt would have been able to teach them easily. There could have been a simple remedy for this difficult situation. For example, participants could have written down their questions on a note card as they thought of them and then passed them to the professor.

If you have trouble hearing, let your audience know. And encourage them to ask their questions in writing, so you can accomplish your goals and meet the needs of your audience.

Ten

The Media

When a reporter sits down at the typewriter, he's nobody's friend.

—THEODORE H. WHITE

The opportunity to present your message through the media—radio, television, newspapers, and magazines—can be either a blessing or a curse. A lively, friendly chat with Katie Couric profiling your new medical procedure on the *Today Show* can send your career into the stratosphere. But if Diane Sawyer is on your case about your company's lack of safety precautions, you may not feel like getting out of bed for a month. One small mention of your product in a national magazine can send your sales soaring, but an ill-advised comment, when recorded in unforgiving black and white, can sink a promising future.

Media attention can make or break products, ideas, campaigns, careers, and even lives. Thus, many major companies spend a great deal of time and money providing their top people with media training. And most large firms have highly detailed policies dictating who is authorized to represent the firm with the media, and when. This is especially important when controversy or disaster strikes and it's imperative that a clear, consistent, accurate, and unassailable message is delivered.

But there are times when *you* could be called on to represent your company to the media—to provide information on a new facility, announce a downsizing, sponsor a charity, present the policy on smoking, announce a new on-site daycare or fitness center, or provide information about progress on the introduction of a product. If your company's leaders have confidence in your ability to represent the firm, chances are you can handle the task. If you are the company leader and decide to be the designated hitter, think about getting an objective opinion about your media-presentability.

While each segment of the media has its own set of rules to follow regarding dress, presentation style, timing, etiquette, and so forth, there are some hard and fast rules that apply universally:

- ALWAYS TELL THE TRUTH. A little fib, or even an exaggeration that makes things more comfortable in the short term, could wind up haunting you in the future.
- Never use irony, sarcasm, or a hostile, defensive tone of voice. There's a good chance your listening or viewing audience won't understand and will pick up the wrong message. And irony or sarcasm rarely translates well into print. Righteous anger can have its place, but you must always remain in control of your anger.
- Never say "No comment." You'll sound like a criminal. If you cannot reasonably answer a question, say, "I don't know, but I'll try to find out for you," or "I'm not in a position to answer that question right now," or "I'm sorry, but that's confidential information."
- Never speak "off the record." Always assume that the mike is still on or that the reporter is still recording your conversation. Most reporters are honest and aboveboard, but there are some investigative types who will do anything to get a story.
- If your media appearance is controversial, don't offer more information than is asked of you.
- Always think in terms of sound bites and headlines. Reporters and editors will comb your presentation for those few words that are attention grabbers. So make your key points in short sentences that will easily translate into a good lead for the evening news. And remember that just about anything you say could be used out of context.

RADIO

Given the choice between a television, radio, or print interview, I'll take radio every time. I'm always much more relaxed during a radio interview, especially one that is taped. Even when a radio segment is live, it's a more comfortable, less stressful climate than television, and you have the luxury of making small slips of the tongue that don't become permanent, the way they do when recorded in print or on video.

One advantage of radio presentations is that it doesn't matter a bit what you look like. You can be having an appallingly bad hair day. That fever blister on your lip can be in full bloom. And your suit can look like you slept in it, which you may have done because it is, after all, 2 a.m.

Another great feature of radio is that you can keep crib sheets, lists, notes, product packaging, and every manner of visual aids piled around you like so many security blankets. You can read directly from the label of the product you are promoting. You can go straight down your list of key points, checking them off as you cover each one. You can even read your own press release. You just can't sound as if that's what you're doing. It's important to keep your tone conversational and to speak clearly with plenty of variety and personality in your voice.

Always keep in mind that your audience cannot see you. Your voice and your choice of words are all the tools you have to express yourself. If you tend to use lots of body language when you speak, look for ways to let your voice give nuance to your words. Instead of shrugging your shoulders or arching an eyebrow, lower or raise your voice. Laugh (but keep it under control—no belly laughs), stretch words out, and pause for emphasis.

You should strive to control the interview without appearing to be aggressive or overbearing. If your interviewer fails to ask the questions that will lead to one of your key points, you can create your own lead by saying, "Your listeners might be interested to know that . . ." or "You might be surprised about . . ."

You can also segue into your key points by linking the interviewer's last point, even if it's a negative one, to one you want to make: "Of course, price is a consideration for most of us, Jerry. Consumers are also looking for quality and value in the products they buy . . ."

Remember that radio people fear dead air. When you stop talking, your interviewer will jump right in and fill the airtime with his or her own chatter. Take ownership of the time.

Here are a few things to keep in mind when you prepare for a radio appearance:

- Use the interviewer's name at the beginning of the interview. You're less likely to forget it during the segment. "Thank you, Ted. I'm delighted to be here this morning." Also use his or her name at the close. "Ted, it was a pleasure to talk with you today." It makes you appear sincere and friendly. But don't overdo the name thing during the interview. Think about how annoying it is when a talk-show guest repeats the host or interviewer's name in every sentence. It sounds phony and insincere, like a direct-marketing sales call for magazines or a lawn service.

- When you are out of town, connect with your listening audience by mentioning their city. "This is my first visit to Denver, and now I know why everyone who has been here has such positive things to say about it."

- Gather your thoughts to answer a question, but don't give up the mike—it's called vamping. "You know, Beth, I'm so glad you've asked that question. It's not one that's asked very often. Though I would like more time to develop a solid response, the current research seems to indicate . . ."

- Never chew gum, suck on candies, or eat during an interview. It is okay to take sips of water, coffee, soda, or tepid tea. In fact, liquids can keep your throat and mouth from feeling dry, and can ward off a cough or froggy voice, which is undesirable when you are on the air.

- If the producer or the interviewer doesn't suggest it first, ask to do a voice test. (Because I have an unusually soft voice, radio technicians often have to adjust the equipment so that my voice and the interviewer's have the same strength. If they don't pick up on it right away, I'll point it out so adjustments don't become a scrambled, last-minute effort.)

- Go over your introduction well in advance of airtime. If there are any discrepancies or if you aren't happy with the intro, be firm about changes. (When I was doing promotional interviews for a toy company, some of the advance material confused my partner's background with mine and indicated that I was the one who had been a teacher. I anticipated this error and made sure it wasn't included in any of the introductions.)

- For a taped interview, remember that it may be edited. (This is less likely in small markets or small stations because their budgets don't allow for much editing.) Make your key points in short sentences and repeat them using different words.

At most radio situations, the interviewer is a talk-show personality. Before an interview, try to review a few of this person's previous segments. Listen to the show several times before you are scheduled to appear. If the radio station is in an out-of-town market, you could ask your public relations consultant, if you have one, to supply you with tapes. You might ask the show's producer for tapes, though you should allow plenty of advance time so that it's not an imposition. Or you can lean on friends who live in that market area. Send them blank tapes to record with or a check to cover the cost, because it is sort of a lot to ask.

Before the interview starts, ask your interviewer a few questions. Is she familiar with your product or service? Would she have a personal interest in what you are promoting or talking about? Where is she from? Does she have kids? Your task is to build rapport in a matter of minutes. You'll need as much information as you can get.

Some interviewers use scripted questions throughout the interview or until the segment gets on a roll. Others are off the cuff right from the beginning. If there is no script, most interviewers don't mind if you suggest questions, as long as you keep them from being blatantly commercial.

Remember that a majority of radio talk shows are scheduled to meet the station's community service requirements (unless it's an all-talk radio station). Thus, the producers, who are often the station's community service directors and the on-air personalities as well, keep interviews as informational and noncommercial as possible. Some even request that you not mention your company or product name on the air. If the show is live, you can slip the name in once or twice, but be subtle. When the show is taped, be prepared for the name to be edited out. Be creative in the way you get your message across when you can't mention specific company or brand names.

Unlike television, which compresses interviews into ludicrously short time segments, radio programming is often broken into fifteen-minute to half-hour time slots, giving you ample time to cover all your key points, mention your product or company name several times without sounding too commercial, plug your book, and thank your mother.

This same feature that makes radio such a positive medium for your presentation is a major drawback if you are on the defensive. Spending a half-hour on the hot seat explaining why you or your company is not responsible for some atrocity is an unpleasant way to spend your time. If you find yourself in this situation, negotiate for a shorter segment, prepare very carefully, stay calm, tell the truth, speak slowly, and pray for it to be over soon.

On a pre-Christmas media tour for VTech Toys, I appeared on a live radio-interview program in a city in the Midwest. While the interviewer was out of the studio, I glanced at the script below his mike. There in black and white, after a perfectly friendly introduction, was his first question: So what makes you a toy expert, anyway?

I was stunned. I'd never been in a confrontational interview situation before. My credentials as an expert on educational toys were based on the fact that I cowrote a syndicated parenting column that focused on home-based educational experiences rather than academic training in the field of education.

Thank God I sneaked a peak at his notes! When he fired that question at me (in a pretty nasty tone, I might add), I was prepared. I explained that most parents are toy experts based on their experience with children and the toys their kids enjoy playing with. Then I added that I had the great opportunity to "play" with thousands of new toys at the International Toy Fair; and through my newspaper column, I heard from parents about toys that pleased them and their children. Finally, I asked him what toys his kids liked (I had already learned about his kids by asking before the interview) and made suggestions about which toys from the product line I was promoting might be of interest to his children. The interview went very well, but I had nightmares about what it would have been like had I been surprised by his lead question.

TELEVISION

In the future, everyone will be famous for 15 minutes.

—ANDY WARHOL

Live television is probably the most intimidating platform for a presentation. The inescapable immediacy, the split-second timing, the intimidating presence of unforgiving cameras, and the possibility that whatever you say or do might be seen by millions of viewers can give even the most experienced presenter a serious case of the jitters.

But television is a powerful, compelling medium. Few other platforms give you the opportunity to advance your message, promote your product, sell your cause, or present your ideas to such a vast audience.

Taped segments, which accompany daily news programming and are the main event for news magazine shows, are equally far reaching, and far more intimidating, because everything you say can be edited and taken out of context. If your taped television presentation is noncontroversial, you have little to worry about. The worst that can happen is that your references to the event, product, cause, or idea you are presenting are edited to exclude references the producer finds too commercial.

Extreme caution is the guiding principle for dealing with controversial issues, however. In an adversarial situation, you'll need to take control as much as possible. Never respond to a negative comment or question by repeating it. Instead, remain confident and positive: "Actually, that's not the case at Stone & Webber, Stan. Our policy has always been to support and assist employees with disabling conditions or diseases." Such a statement should deflate or at least deflect an attack. Of course, your response must always be truthful; make sure you can back it up at a later date.

PR people around the country spend their entire working lives placing clients on television, and with the enormous expansion of cable, opportunities for television appearances have grown exponentially. Today, your chances of making a presentation on television are far greater than they were ten or even five years ago.

There are consultants whose sole service is to train executives and company representatives for television appearances. Most often the training takes the form of role playing in front of a video camera followed by a blow-by-blow critique. The experts point out that the tilt of your head looks exaggerated, that your fidgeting hands are distracting, that your jacket bunches across your shoulders, that you say "um" between every other word, or that your hair obscures your eyes.

During my own TV training, I was shocked at how washed out and pale I looked. My graying, too-long hair seemed to blend in with my skin, and my eyebrows were barely detectable. The consultants were kind, but firm. I cut and colored my hair and wore more makeup for my television appearances. I was much happier about the way I looked after my mini-makeover. Also, knowing that I looked reasonably attractive on television greatly increased my confidence.

But a television appearance is about much more than the way you look. Because TV segments on news and talk shows are short—ranging from thirty seconds to six minutes or so—you have scant time to make your presentation. It's absolutely critical that you keep the interview focused on your key points. But it's not always easy.

For example, say you are booked to appear on *Good Morning Dallas* to promote an early childhood vaccination program. You have three minutes to explain the importance of the program and how the audience can participate in it. But when the host introduces you, he goes off on a riff about his own bout with chicken pox as a kid, using up your valuable airtime. You have to take control. As soon as he pauses for a breath, you grab that control by relating to his experience with a startling fact. You say, "Well Ron, as bad as your experience was, it's far worse—actually deadly—for hundreds of children every year. And those deaths can be prevented."

Decide in advance what one point is the most important and make that key point immediately. You'll rarely have time to go into much detail, so stick to your key message, adding one or two other key points if you find that time permits.

It's not unusual for the producer to tell you at the time your appearance is booked that you'll do a five- or six-minute segment, only to reduce the segment to two minutes just before airtime. In this case, you'll have to quickly rethink your presentation, drop details, and just present your message. There won't be time for embellishments.

Here are some tips that can help your TV presentation:

- Become familiar with the format and the on-air personalities of the show you will appear on, if it's possible. If you can't get tapes of the show yourself, ask your PR firm to do it for you. There are also media companies that will provide this service.
- If your presentation includes an 800 number, an address, or other information that viewers will want to retain, be sure to let the producer know about it when the segment is booked. Ask them to make a visual of your address or phone number to go on the screen while you repeat it. It's been my experience that more often than not, the studio staff is unaware of the need for a visual. Sometimes they will scramble to create one, but usually there just isn't time. In local markets, I always give a copy of the information to the station's receptionist, who usually answers the phone too. He or she will then have the 800 number or address to provide viewers who call in for the information.
- If you'd like to show a video clip, inform the producer at the time of the booking and send a copy of the clip (be sure it's very short, only a few seconds) to him or her at least two weeks prior to your appearance. Make a reminder phone call a week before, and another one the day before, your appearance.
- When you schedule your television appearance, ask how long the segment will be, but be prepared for that to change minutes before airtime.

- Always arrive well before airtime. In most cases the producer will tell you when to arrive. If not, ask. It's far better to arrive a half hour earlier than necessary than to rush in at the last minute. (In one instance, I replaced a guest who was a no-show, and was granted double airtime. Because I had arrived early, I was relaxed, and ready to go on short notice.)

- In a one-on-one interview situation, your interviewer will look at the camera, but you must keep your eyes on the interviewer. He or she is the "contact" for the viewing audience.

- If you are interviewed by two people, which is frequently the case in talk-show formats, be sure you sit or stand to one side of the team rather than between them. When you are placed in the middle, you'll find yourself turning back and forth to address one then the other, which makes you look like you're watching a tennis match.

- If you have long hair, wear it away from your face so that the viewing audience can see your mouth and eyes.

- Don't wear clunky, showy jewelry that will make noise, catch the light, or cause other distractions. (If your presentation is about clunky jewelry, ignore this tip.)

- Keep in mind that your microphone will be attached to your clothing. Usually the wire is run up under your jacket and attached at the lapel. If you aren't wearing a suit jacket, the wire can run under your blouse or shirt and come out between the buttons below your chin. Big scarves can get in the way, as can jewelry. Once the mike is in place and the technician has tested the sound levels, ignore it and speak normally.

- In a sofa-and-chair talk-show set, the camera will show you from head to toe at some point, so be aware of how your legs are crossed. Women should cross their legs to the side at the ankles; men should cross them at the knee, but not with the heel on the knee; or keep them parallel and uncrossed and turned lightly to the side.

- Dresses and skirts should be long enough to cover your thighs; exposed knees are okay unless you are very heavy.
- Trousers should not hike up to midcalf when you are seated. Check to make sure that bare skin doesn't show above the top of your socks. If the venue is somewhat informal, women may wear trousers as long as they aren't too tight. Stockings should be the same color as the trousers.
- Shoes should be polished. Though they don't always show, don't risk looking scruffy.
- Your clothing style will depend on what it is you are presenting. A business suit is almost always appropriate, unless you are demonstrating a physical activity or your presentation includes some kind of costume or uniform. On television, dark colors—especially red, blue, and green—look better than lighter shades. Pure white is usually too harsh, although a white blouse or shirt under a suit jacket is acceptable as long as it's not shiny. And large prints, wide stripes, and oversized polka dots have an undesirable dizzying effect.
- Women should consider wearing slightly more makeup than in their normal day-time look, unless that look is already heavily madeup. Use some powder or matte-finish foundation to avoid a shiny forehead, nose, and chin. Highlight the cheeks with blush, and diminish a double chin with a faint and well-blended line of blush from just under the chin down the throat. Lips can be defined using a dark-colored lipstick applied as an outline with a lip brush or pencil, with a slightly lighter color filling in the lips. You may want to use more mascara than normal, but use restraint with eyeliner and shadow to avoid looking like a raccoon. Check your teeth for stray lipstick.

Men generally use little or no makeup for television appearances unless their skin is extremely shiny or they have unusually heavy beards. Sometimes a bald pate needs a light application of face powder or matte foundation to avoid shine. Ask the producer if a makeup artist will help you out or if you'll have to do it yourself.

- Don't experiment with a new hairstyle or hair color just before a television presentation. If you need a haircut, have it done three to five days before your appearance. Women often have their hair coiffed, not cut, just prior to a TV appearance, but this may not be feasible for an early morning segment.

- Try to move around while you are waiting your turn to appear. Sitting still while others are on the air can bring on a serious case of the jitters. Just before you start your segment, flap your arms, windmill them in big circles, and bounce up and down on your toes a few times to get your circulation moving. Breathe deeply (but don't hyperventilate), and relax your neck and shoulders.

- Smile. Don't grin, because it will look like a grimace. Show your teeth, and relax your jaw.

- Keep your head straight, and avoid tilting it to one side. Tilting makes you look less sure of yourself.

- Lean forward from the waist slightly. In a side-chair or sofa setup, fold your hands loosely in your lap. You may use a few small hand gestures, but don't wave your arms around. Keep your arms naturally at your sides; don't rest your elbows on the arms of the chair. If you are seated at the news desk, fold your hands neatly on the desk surface in front of you, but keep them loose and not in fists.

- If you are demonstrating a product, avoid covering an important feature with your hands. It helps to check with the camera technicians before your presentation about the best angle to hold your product or visual aid so that it won't cause glare.

Contrary to what most first-time TV presenters expect, you rarely wait in a fancy "green room" feasting on donuts and coffee before your appearance, and you are usually on your own for your makeup and hair. With the occasional exception and unlike most national show facilities, most local-market television studios don't have a special room with makeup artists and hairstylists waiting to do their magic. At some stations, I've found nothing more than a small table with a mirror, a hair brush, and a can of hair spray tucked in a corner of the studio behind one of the sets. At others, the ladies' room doubles as the makeup room. And it's definitely B.Y.O.

The "green room," which got its name from the color of the walls in the guest waiting room in the early years of the *Tonight Show*, is often not a room at all. It can refer to a hallway, the producer's office, a corner of the studio, or even the control room. It's almost always cold and dark, and, if it's in the studio, you have to keep very still and quiet because they are taping or on the air.

NEWSPAPERS AND MAGAZINES

Reporters are like alligators. You don't have to love them, you don't necessarily have to like them. But you do have to feed them.

—ANONYMOUS

There are essentially two kinds of newspaper interviews—fluff and investigative. The fluff pieces are always positive. The investigative ones are often hostile. This is a gross generalization, of course, but it's a good idea to keep this generality in mind.

In the old, pre-electronic media days, public relations people spent their business lives getting favorable "press" for their clients. This meant cultivating relationships with editors and reporters, and sending out press releases and media advisories. PR consultants did their best to position their clients as experts in their fields and would encourage reporters to look to the clients for comments, opinions, and background information to fill out their stories.

Though the electronic media is a major force, newspapers and magazines still command large readerships and are vitally important.

A good reporter or feature writer often gathers far more information than he or she is able to use in an article. Interview subjects might answer dozens of questions and wind up as a half-sentence reference somewhere on page 52.

In nearly every story I have placed as a public relations consultant, I have found at least one error in reporting. And during my stint as a press secretary and my own forays into local civic and political activities, I have been repeatedly annoyed, even appalled, by how reporters have interpreted the things they write about. Sometimes I've wondered if the reporter and I had actually attended the same meeting.

As a result of my experiences, I have developed a certain skepticism about the media, especially newspapers. And I rarely take something I've read or seen in the media as gospel truth. However, many people get much of their local and regional news from newspapers, which remain a major communications tool.

Therefore, it is necessary to be prepared for a reporter's errors. These mistakes are rarely intentional; they are usually a result of tight deadlines and inadequate note taking.

Here are a few tips to help you present well in a print interview:

- Offer the interviewer some hard-copy background information. Most reporters are overworked and have tight deadlines, so they appreciate having some of the research done for them. This is especially important if your presentation includes lots of numbers, important dates, and technological or industry-specific information. Written background information is less apt to be as appreciated by an investigative reporter doing a controversial story.

- Try to have your interview face to face. A reporter often gathers information by phone, but unless he or she is looking for a quick fact or a confirmation, it's better to do it in person. You may want to stage your interview on your turf, in a conference room or your office, for example. Be sure there are no distractions or interruptions that will disrupt your train of thought or prevent the reporter from accurately hearing what you have to say.

- If your story is controversial or involves difficult-to-understand language or concepts, avoid scheduling a lunch or dinner interview. Restaurants are full of distractions, and you are likely to get off track, and the reporter will probably miss something important.

- If there is even an ounce of controversy in your story, bring along a tape recorder and use it. There's always a chance you will have to prove you said something other than what was reported. Always let the reporter know you are taping. If he or she doesn't like the idea, which is unlikely, don't do the interview.

- Speak slowly and clearly. Pause to spell names or unusual words. Repeat figures or dates, and wait for the reporter to write them down.

- A newspaper or magazine news piece or feature article will likely be long enough to include a fair amount of detail. Your task is to provide details to support your key points, rather than to move further afield.

In 1976 I was interviewed by a reporter for a local weekly paper about the small house museum I was running. While the interview was positive and friendly, I was horribly embarrassed when I read the news piece. The reporter

---

> quoted me verbatim; and at one point, in explaining how supportive the community had been in providing furnishings for the museum, I said something like "And all these wonderful people have done such wonderful things." It must have sounded empty-headed and vapid, and it read even more so. The moral of this story is "Always, always, ALWAYS think before you speak to a reporter."

IN-HOUSE VIDEO

Video presentations for internal distribution have become such a widespread communications tool that many companies have fully staffed in-house studios to prepare them. Taped presentations are particularly effective for large organizations in which key executives must communicate with large numbers of employees and for companies whose employees and representatives are located in sites other than corporate headquarters.

Insurance companies prepare video presentations to inform their agents about new products and policies. New hires for national companies learn about the corporate culture and practices through video presentations. Training sessions on subjects as diverse as time management, safety regulations, pension planning, and dealing with diversity are delivered via video.

If your job includes making video presentations, the section on commercial television appearances in this chapter should be helpful. The main difference is that corporate videos allow you more control over the content and the editing process. You may actually prepare a script. There won't be trick questions, the need to wrest control from a dizzy interviewer, or the need to compress your message into an unrealistically short time frame.

Another difference is that instead of addressing the viewer through the interviewer, you look directly into the camera. Use plenty of personality in your voice, vary the tempo of your speech, and keep your hand gestures under control. If you have a prepared script, rehearse it thoroughly, not to memorize it, but so that you can read from the Tele-Promp-Ter fluently and with expression.

Quotations for Speeches

Presenters find it's helpful to borrow the words of others to begin or close their remarks, to make a point, or to add a little humor or poignancy. Good presenters keep a stash of pithy or pointed quotations to put some spice into their mix of words. This appendix provides you with a diverse collection of quotations, sayings, and nuggets.

When using a quotation, you may want to introduce it with one of the following phrases:

- A wise person once said . . .
- (Name of person quoted) once said . . .
- I read that . . .
- I've heard that . . .
- Someone once said . . .

Some quotations contain somewhat archaic or stilted language. And older quotations often contain the words *he, him, man,* and so forth, making them potentially offensive to those who are sensitive to gender bias in language. The Task Force on Bias-Free Language suggests that direct quotes should not be altered in scholarly writing. But the members of the task force also understand that this is a problem for those writers who use quotations that contain biased language.

Since this book is not specifically geared to the scholarly presenter, I suggest that careful editing be applied to these witty, sage, or insightful quotations so that they will fit your needs. I have taken the liberty of changing some of the quotations listed in this appendix in an effort to pass along words that will not offend. (The edited quotations are marked with an asterisk.)

If you feel the need to acknowledge any changes you make in someone's quotation, you might say:

- (Name) once offered this advice.
- I read something that impressed me. It goes something like this.
- There's an old saying that goes something like this.
- To paraphrase (name) . . .

It is my hope that a few of the following quotations will be appropriate for your presentation and will enhance what you have to say:

> *The world judges you by what you have done,*
> *not by what you have started out to do; by what*
> *you have completed, not by what you have*
> *begun. The bulldog wins by the simple expedient*
> *of holding on to the finish.*
>
> —BALTASAR GRACIAN

> *The first principle of achievement is mental*
> *attitude. People begin to achieve when they*
> *begin to believe.*
>
> —J. C. ROBERTS

1. Do more than exist, live.
2. Do more than touch, feel.
3. Do more than look, observe.
4. Do more than read, absorb.
5. Do more than hear, listen.
6. Do more than listen, understand.

7. Do more than think, ponder.
8. Do more than talk, say something.
—JOHN H. RHOADES

Measure twice, saw once.
—ANONYMOUS

Talk low, talk slow and don't say too much.
—TEXAS BIX BINDER

No one is more confusing than the person who gives good advice while setting a bad example.
—ANONYMOUS

I have learned that success is to be measured not so much by the position that one has reached, as by the obstacles which he has overcome while trying to succeed.
—BOOKER T. WASHINGTON

You never know what is enough until you know what is more than enough.
—WILLIAM BLAKE

Chance favors the prepared mind.
—LOUIS PASTEUR

The obvious is that which is never seen until someone expresses it simply.
—KAHLIL GIBRAN

A vocabulary of truth and simplicity will be of service throughout life.

—WINSTON CHURCHILL

We boil at different degrees.

—RALPH WALDO EMERSON

What is easy is seldom excellent.

—SAMUEL JOHNSON

A sense of humor is a sense of proportion.

—KAHLIL GIBRAN

Funny how people despise platitudes, when they are usually the truest thing going. A thing has to be pretty true before it gets to be a platitude.

—KATHARINE F. GEROULD

Time has no divisions to make its passage. There is never a thunderstorm or blare of trumpets to announce the beginning of a new month or year. Even when a new century begins, it is only we mortals who ring bells . . .

—THOMAS MANN

Always do right; this will gratify some people and astonish the rest.

—MARK TWAIN

I praise loudly; I blame softly.
—CATHERINE II OF RUSSIA

No one ever makes us mad. We grow angry as a result of our own choice.
—ANONYMOUS

The torrid sun melts mountain snows.
When anger comes, then wisdom goes.
—CHINESE SAYING

Swallowing angry words is better than choking on an apology.
—ANONYMOUS

There are no great people; only great challenges that ordinary people are forced by circumstances to meet.
—ANONYMOUS

Happiness adds and multiplies as we divide it with others.
—ANONYMOUS

Never bend your head. Always hold it high.
Look the world straight in the eye.
—HELEN KELLER

*By appreciation we make excellence in others
our own property.*
—VOLTAIRE

*The power of persistence, of enduring defeat
and of gaining victory by defeats, is one of those
forces which never loses its charm.*
—RALPH WALDO EMERSON

*The most difficult thing in the world is to
appreciate what we have—until we lose it.*
—ANONYMOUS

*The strongest words are often used in the
weakest arguments.*
—ANONYMOUS

*After eating an entire bull, a mountain lion felt
so good he started roaring. He kept it up until a
hunter came along and shot him. The moral:
When you're full of bull, keep your mouth shut.*
—TEXAS BIX BINDER

*He has achieved success who has lived well,
laughed often and loved much.*
—BESSIE ANDERSON

There is no sin except stupidity.
—OSCAR WILDE

In this world there are only two tragedies. One is not getting what one wants, and the other is getting it.

—OSCAR WILDE

I am seeking only to face realities and to face them without soft concealments.

—WOODROW WILSON

If we want a thing badly enough, we can make it happen. If we let ourselves be discouraged, that is proof that our wanting was inadequate.

—DOROTHY SAYERS

Read every day something no one else is reading. Think something no one else is thinking. It is bad for the mind to be always a part of unanimity.

—CHRISTOPHER MORLEY

As a rule indeed, grown-up people are fairly correct on matters of fact; it is in the higher gift of imagination that they are so sadly to seek.

—KENNETH GRAHAME

Those who bring sunshine to the lives of others cannot keep it from themselves.

—JAMES BARRIE

*When there are two people in a business who
always agree, one of them is unnecessary.*
—WILLIAM WRIGLEY, JR.

*The easiest way to eat crow is while it's still
warm. The colder it gets, the harder it is to
swaller.*
—TEXAS BIX BINDER

You ain't heard nothin' yet, folks.
—AL JOLSON

*They say that life is a highway and its
milestones are the years.*
—JOYCE KILMER

*Diplomacy is to do and say
The nastiest thing in the nicest way.*
—ISAAC GOLDBERG

*Politics is the science of how who gets what,
when and why.*
—SIDNEY HILLMAN

*I'd rather have an inch of dog than miles of
pedigree.*
—DANA BURNET

*Nothing changes more constantly than the past;
for the past that influences our lives does not
consist of what actually happened, but of what
we believe happened.**

—GERALD WHITE JOHNSON

*Each honest calling, each walk of life, has its
own elite, its own aristocracy based on
excellence of performance.*

—JAMES BRYANT CONANT

Believe it or not.

—ROBERT RIPLEY

*Baloney is flattery so thick it cannot be true,
and blarney is flattery so thin we like it.*

—FULTON JOHN SHEEN

*I had to sink my yacht to make my guests go
home.*

—F. SCOTT FITZGERALD

*If you find yourself in a hole, the first thing to
do is stop diggin'.*

—TEXAS BIX BINDER

*The way of the future is coming and there is no
fighting it.*

—ANNE MORROW LINDBERGH

What is past is prologue.
—WILLIAM SHAKESPEARE

I hate quotations! Tell me what you know.
—RALPH WALDO EMERSON

When you have eliminated the impossible,
whatever remains, however improbable, must be
the truth.
—SIR ARTHUR CONAN DOYLE

The human body is an instrument for the
production of art in the life of the human soul.
—ALFRED NORTH WHITEHEAD

The materials of action are variable, but the use
we make of them should be constant.
—EPICTETUS (C. 60 A.D.)

Remember this, that there is a proper dignity
and proportion to be observed in the
performance of every action in life.
—MARCUS AURELIUS

Look beneath the surface; let not the several
qualities of a thing nor its worth escape thee.
—MARCUS AURELIUS

Look to the essence of a thing, whether it be a
point of doctrine, of practise, or of
intrepretation.
—MARCUS AURELIUS

Never invest your money in anything that eats or needs repainting.

—BILLY ROSE

If a man has good corn or wood or boards or pigs to sell, or can make better chairs or knives, crucibles, or church organs, than anybody else, you will find a broad, hard-beaten path to his house, though it be in the woods.

—RALPH WALDO EMERSON

It is better to ask some of the questions than to know all the answers.

—JAMES THURBER

There are six big reasons why people find their way into top management positions:

They know how to manage others.

They know how to read what is behind the figures of the business.

They think simply.

Problems never take them by surprise.

They have imagination about the public.

They have faith in human nature.

—ROBERT R. UPDEGRAFF

There would be plenty of sympathy if people would spread it around instead of using it all on themselves.

—ANONYMOUS

Tact fails the moment it is noticed.
—EDWARD LONGSTRETH

*If the power to do hard work is not talent, it is
the best possible substitute for it.*
—ANONYMOUS

*A teacher who is attempting to teach without
inspiring the pupil with a desire to learn is
hammering on cold iron.*
—HORACE MANN

The giant oak is an acorn that held its ground.
—ANONYMOUS

*Lose an hour in the morning and you will be
looking for it the rest of the day.*
—LORD CHESTERFIELD

*Remember, even a kick in the caboose is a step
forward.*
—TEXAS BIX BINDER

*No man-made weapon has been devised so
lethal, potent or dangerous as words wrongly
used.*
—LARRY DORST

*Happiness makes up in height for what it lacks
in length.*
—ROBERT FROST

Speed is good when wisdom clears the way.
—EDWARD R. MURROW

Hell is truth seen too late.
—ALEXANDER ADAM

I leave this rule for others when I'm dead,
Be always sure you're right—then go ahead.
—DAVY CROCKETT

If life had a second edition, how I would
correct the proofs.
—JOHN CLARE

All work is as seed sown; it grows and spreads,
and sows itself anew.
—THOMAS CARLYLE

Nothing great was ever achieved without
enthusiasm.
—RALPH WALDO EMERSON

Dogmatism is puppyism come to its full growth.
—DOUGLAS JERROLD

Never ask a barber if he thinks you need a
haircut.
—TEXAS BIX BINDER

It is much easier to be critical than to be correct.

—BENJAMIN DISRAELI

If you call a tail a leg, how many legs has a dog? Five? No; calling a tail a leg don't make it a leg.

—ABRAHAM LINCOLN

After the verb "To Love," "To Help" is the most beautiful verb in the world.

—BARONESS BERTHA VON SUTTNER

Even a thought, even a possibility can shatter us and transform us.

—FRIEDRICH WILHELM NIETZSCHE

To know is nothing at all; to imagine is everything.

—ANATOLE FRANCE

It is difference of opinion that makes horse races.

—MARK TWAIN

A classic is something that everybody wants to have read and nobody wants to read.

—MARK TWAIN

*If you hit a pony over the nose at the outset of
your acquaintance, he may not love you, but he
will take a deep interest in your movements
ever afterwards.*

—RUDYARD KIPLING

Luck is good when it isn't bad.

—ANONYMOUS

*Paying attention to simple little things that most
people neglect makes a few people rich.*

—HENRY FORD

*All life is an experiment. The more experiments
you make, the better.*

—RALPH WALDO EMERSON

Index

McArdle, Geri E.H., 75
*McGraw-Hill 36-Hour Course:
Business Presentations*
(Arrendondo), 80
Magazines, 186-189
Mailing list, building, 134
Make-up, 184-185
*Making Successful Presentations—
A Self-Teaching Guide* (Smith), 41
Maslow's hierarchy of needs, 20-21
Meals. *See* Food
Media, 9, 173-189
rules for dealing with, 174
Microphones, 106-108, 183
Microsoft, 78
Mind Map, 40, 45-46
Motivation, of audience, 19, 50
Motivational presentations, 9
Multimedia presentations, 86-88
Multipurpose presentations, 4

Names, remembering, 56, 176
Nelson, Robert, 49
Never Be Nervous Again
(Sarnoff), 149
Newspapers, 186-189
New York Times, 59

Ober, Scott, 2, 21, 162
Office suites, 98
Older people, speaking to, 165-166
One-on-a-roomful rapport, 57-58
One-on-a-table rapport, 56-57
One-on-one rapport, 54-56
Opening, of presentation, 46-48
Outlines, 41-44
Overhead transparencies, 84-85

Panel discussions, 160-161
Passive voice, 122-123
Performance Improvement, 146-147
Perot, Ross, 6-7
Persons, Hal, 66, 140, 143
Persuasion (software), 78
Persuasive presentations, 2-3
format for, 33-34
organization of, 49-50

parts of, 32-33
Peterson, Houston, *xiv*
Pickens, James W., 124
Pitch, of voice, 72, 141-144
Podiums, 106
Political presentations, 6-7
PowerPoint (software), 78
Pragmatic audience, 15-16
Presentation Primer, The (Nelson
and Wallick), 49
Presentations
how to deliver, 65-73
impromptu, 155-157
logistics of, 93-120
organization of, 31-52
types of, 1-11
Presentation (software), 78
Problem-solving approach to
organization, 38, 48
Pro/con approach to organization,
38-39, 48
Promptness, importance of, 115-118
Props, 91-92
Psychological progression model,
and organization, 49

Questionnaires, 137-138
Questions
asking of audience, 57-58
handling negative, 180
Questions and answer period
maintaining control of, 23-27
rules for, 27
stock phrases for, 28
Quotations, for speeches, 191-205

Radio, 175-179
Rapport, with audience, 46, 54-58
Reader's Digest, 59
Reading, of speech, 65-66
Reagan, Ronald, 59
Redundancies, 127-128
Research, 39
Rickles, Don, 59
Roberts, Dave, 87

Sales presentations, 4-5

FIND MORE ON THIS TOPIC BY VISITING
BusinessTown.com
The Web's big site for growing businesses!

- ☑ Separate channels on all aspects of starting and running a business
- ☑ Lots of info on how to do business online
- ☑ 1,000+ pages of savvy business advice
- ☑ Complete web guide to thousands of useful business sites
- ☑ Free e-mail newsletter
- ☑ Question and answer forums, and more!

businesstown.com